Home Work

Home Work

essays on love and housekeeping

Helen Hayward

PUNCHER & WATTMANN

First published in 2023
Published by Puncher and Wattmann
PO Box 279
Waratah NSW 2298

https://www.puncherandwattmann.com
web@puncherandwattmann.com

ISBN   9781922571915

Cover image design by Charlie Armstrong
Cover design by Miranda Douglas Designs
Editing by Ed Wright
Proofreading by Clara Davidson
Typesetting by Morgan Arnett
Printed by Lightning Source International

 A catalogue record for this
book is available from the
NATIONAL
LIBRARY National Library of Australia
OF AUSTRALIA

Contents

foreword

We might be tempted to feel rather sorry for someone who confessed that their greatest pleasure in life was staying at home – or worse, that their deepest satisfactions sprang from what (usually with a sneer) we call 'housekeeping'. What would need to have gone wrong for someone to prefer their own bedroom or kitchen to the theatres and clubs, parties and conference venues of the world? How narrow would someone's horizons need to have grown for them to devote an hour to choosing a gift for a friend, or a lamp for the living room? Our era has a hard time maintaining sympathy for domesticity. Reality lies outside our doors. There are really only two categories of people who can be forgiven for being heavily invested in spending time at home: small children. And losers.

But after launching our ambitions on the high seas, after trying for a few decades to make a mark on our times, after exhausting ourselves sucking up to those in power and coping with gossip, slander and scandal, we might start to think less harshly of those who prefer to remain within their own walls and think a lot – and with pride – about sewing projects and recipes, seedlings and garlic crushers, laundry cupboards and cleaning products.

It might, of course, be preferable to manage to bend the world to one's own will, to tidy up the minds of millions or to fashion a business in one's image. But after a bit of time on the planet, some of us may be ready to look with new understanding and admiration at those who can draw satisfaction from making blackberry jam, taking strikings from lavender or painting the bedroom floor.

This is where Helen Hayward's luminous book comes in. She encourages us to look with greater generosity, and newfound interest, at the domestic side of our lives – and to see in the management of a home one of the great triumphs and challenges of existence. We know – of course – that we have to pay the bills, clean up, manage the laundry, make the bed, cook some meals, keep the fridge stocked and take out the rubbish. These issues take up a lot of our attention and time anyway, but they are rarely at the core of what we think a good life is about. Yet the notion that practical matters have no legitimate place in our days and nights makes our lives far harder than they need to be. We get irritated by what seem like maddeningly minor details. Should we be taking clothes to the dry cleaner? Should we have a roster for taking out the bins? What to do about storage jars? But not only are we annoyed. We're annoyed that we end up annoyed about things that seem so utterly petty.

Frustration doesn't just stem from things being difficult, it stems from them being unexpected and difficult. Nobody complains that it's quite hard to climb Mount Everest. But our culture has for decades encouraged the idea that domestic matters are beneath the dignity of the sophisticated individual: we should be out working or having fun. We under-budget for domestic issues and feel that they shouldn't be things we have to take up again and again. When we understand that an issue is important and complex, we take it for granted there will be friction that will take time to clear up, that there will need to be a lot of explanation, negotiation and debate. The small, bounded, repetitive tasks of domestic life in fact play a great part in the essential task of living well. The great themes come into focus in them. With Helen Hayward's help, we can accept the fundamental dignity of the ironing board and the store cupboard, the kitchen and the bathroom.

Maybe housekeeping is a consolation – or home work, as Hayward has come to understand it. So be it. We might once have wanted to tame and educate the entire world, to have had millions of people agree with us and to gain the adulation of strangers. But such plans are inherently unstable and open to being destroyed by envy and vanity. This book shows us how a devotion to home can shore up our moods if our wider surroundings grow hostile. We can reactivate our dormant appreciation of our surroundings and find meaning in nothing greater or smaller than sewing on a few buttons in the late evening or choosing a new fabric for a chair. Hayward is not naive, she understands how war, politics and business work, but it is precisely because she does so that she is keen to throw her spotlight elsewhere. Her writing is – in the deep sense – political, in that it articulates a vision of how we might ideally live, and covertly criticises military generals and power-hungry politicians, business leaders and actors. It hints that waving flags at rallies and sounding important at meetings is well and good, but that the true battles and successes lie elsewhere, in the challenges of daily life, of so-called ordinary existence.

With Hayward as our guide, tonight, we might – once more – choose to stay in, do some reading, patch a hole in a sweater, try a new arrangement for the living room and be intensely grateful that we have overcome the wish to live too much in the minds of strangers.

Alain de Botton
London 2023

introduction

Whenever I answer the door wearing an apron, the person on the doorstep looks me up and down. What's normal for me, protecting my clothes as I tip stock into a colander, mix dough and mop floors, seems less so for others. Wearing an apron to the front door in the late afternoon seems as provocative as opening it in my pyjamas in the early morning.

I didn't start out in life wearing an apron. As a girl, I hardly thought about my home, which I mostly took for granted. Whenever it did cross my mind, I sided with the author Rose McAuley who claimed that 'a well-kept house is a sign of a misspent life'. Domestic life was a tangle of repetitive, unfulfilling tasks that paid work was designed to release people from. Like all my friends, I assumed that caring about the home meant avoiding the real challenges of life. So completely did I think this, I rarely heard this side of life mentioned. Domesticity just went without saying. And if ever the topic did come up, I scoffed at the idea that running a home – growing vegetables, cooking for friends, renovating – might one day fill me with pride.

On leaving Australia for London, after an arts degree in my home town of Adelaide, I felt confident that the woman I hoped to become would emerge through my career, my self-esteem growing as I met the demands of the world. A string of shared flats, north and south of the Thames, were merely the backdrop to my working life. It wasn't until I moved into a studio flat, in my late 20s, that the place where I lived helped to make sense of my life beyond it. Only then did I stop for long enough to realise that what I'd left Adelaide to escape, the comforts of home, weren't to be despised.

Still, I continued to run away from housekeeping for five more years, during which time I met Paul, the man I would give my heart to. Until one day, halfway through my 30s, there was nowhere to hide. Until, that is, I became a mother. From day one of motherhood, the emotional, imaginative and physical work of looking after my baby and home felt demanding. I felt I had no choice but to stay on top of household tasks. They could no longer be put off till the weekend. If I wanted to look forward to getting out of bed each morning – and to do anything, really, over and above looking after my baby when I did – I had to prioritise housekeeping. Laundry, cooking, organising, errands, shopping and cleaning, became urgent. My life may not have depended on them, but my sanity and wellbeing did. Besides, it was never just the tasks themselves. Looking after my home always involved more than keeping it clean and tidy. What felt demanding was something larger and more encompassing that didn't have a name and that, over the years, I've come to think of as home work.

Caring for my home in an intelligent way, creating a pleasant atmosphere there, keeping surfaces clean and tidy, and expressing the love that makes sense of this whole endeavour – these didn't happen by magic. No matter what was going on in other parts of my life, home work demanded time, thought, creativity, love and effort. Without these things, home was a dull, squib thing. With them it felt bright and plump.

By the time Paul and I had our second child, I'd come to accept that there is an art to running a home. A warm and attractive living space doesn't happen naturally. If anything, the opposite. A pleasant, welcoming home is an achievement that assumes hundreds of smaller efforts in support of this ideal. The problem, for me, was that in my heart I wasn't convinced these efforts were worth making. How could homely satisfactions like cooking, gardening and DIY hold their own against foot-on-the-ladder, worldly strivings? If I gave in to my desire for home-cooked meals, line-dried sheets and a lively garden, mightn't I disappear like Alice down the rabbit hole?

Around the time my kids reached the ages of two and four, I did just that, returning to Melbourne with my family in search of a better quality of life than seemed possible for us in London. I felt excited about moving back to Australia. It was what I'd been longing for. But then, within a year of moving out of a first-floor flat in London into a house with a garden in Melbourne, I developed a fear of being at home. I felt overwhelmed by everything there was to do there. Where to start? I'd gotten what I wanted: a family, a house and interesting part-time work. Yet I missed the pre-child me. The woman who knew what she was doing, and what she was about, between 9 and 4 on weekdays – the scheduled me. Teaching part-time became code for spending the afternoon chasing my tail at home. Bossed about by everything I felt I should be doing, time slipped like sand through my fingers, the big hand on the kitchen clock whizzed mockingly around its face. Should I be pairing socks or calling my elderly aunt? Preparing dinner or checking my diary? Taking my kids to the park or fixing the sprinkler out the back? Feeding the worms or vacuuming the floors?

It was at this point, tired of splattering olive oil on my clothes, that I bought my first apron. Doing up this black linen apron had an instant effect. I immediately felt less stressed. I still brought in the washing and prepared dinner. However, wearing this apron stopped the chatter in my head that told me I should be doing something – anything – else. I didn't drop by my desk to check on the emails I wasn't sending or the writing I wasn't doing. I just got on with whatever needed attending to around the house, and then felt better for having done it. Because until I took off my apron, my focus was on home work.

Whenever anyone asked me the 'What do you do?' question, I'd say that I was a writer and teacher. It was true. I did write every day and taught part time. However, only rarely did I mention my job. This was because my job seemed less acceptable, less noteworthy than my writing and teaching work, even though it could be equally challenging, time consuming and interesting. My job stretched and inspired me. It had long hours, low status and was unregulated. It wasn't quite a calling, though some days it felt like one. My job – and don't get me wrong, I put my hand up for this – was to keep our home running smoothly without shouting or moaning too much. My job was housekeeping.

It wasn't just me. I knew countless people – not all of them women – who did the lion's share of keeping their homes running smoothly without shouting or moaning too much. They may not have felt called to it, as I did. They may not have treated it as a job, nor wear an apron doing it. Still, they spent a similar amount of time shopping, cleaning, cooking, organising and maintaining things, and generally making things happen at home. And then clearing up afterwards. Like me, they didn't consider this their main work. Certainly, the world didn't. Perhaps this was why the subject of domesticity was glossed over in conversation. Mostly, we just got on and did it. Yet measured in hours, devotion, effort and skill, it made up a big part, up to a quarter, of our waking hours, especially for those of us with families.

So what exactly is housekeeping – or home work as I've come to think of it? Home work is the sum of all our longings and efforts at home. It's seeking a level of order that we never quite achieve. It's caring about a raft of things that we otherwise wouldn't care about were it not for our desire for and commitment to a pleasant home.

Home work takes in three overlapping spheres: the domestic arts (cooking, gardening, craft, renovating), housekeeping (the hundred-and-one tasks that add up to a well-run home) and housework (cleaning). Then there is love. Love is the glue that holds together the everything that there is to do at home. Without love, there wouldn't be much point, bar survival, in all our domestic efforts. Home work is the whole constant, insane, wonderful juggle of keeping up a home worth loving.

Home work is demanding because it consumes real energy and takes place in real time. The upside, often overlooked, is that with the right attitude it can be energising and grounding. At the end of the day, which is when most of us do our home work, it helps keep us sane and gives us something important back.

Home work is also an attitude, an approach to life that encompasses everything that goes into how we live our lives. This is how it goes for me. It's sharing a family bathroom with a thought for the person who might use it next. It's having a reusable bag at the supermarket check-out. It's remembering a loved one's birthday and thinking about how to celebrate it ahead of time. It's banging the sink strainers into the bin straight after washing up. It's digging a hole in the garden before the plant I fell for in the nursery gets root-bound in its pot. It's hanging doonas on the line because it's a sunny day. It's having the right ingredients for dinner in the fridge, and marinating meat overnight. It's picking herbs as I pass through the garden, knowing how much I hate fetching them in the dark. It's borrowing cookery books from the library when I tire of my own cooking. It's folding tea towels straight off the line because it's heartening to open the drawer to a neat stack. It's taking a sewing class after despairing of not being able to fit a zip. It's stashing chicken bones in the freezer and remembering to defrost the stock that I go on to make from them. It's filling hot water bottles on cold nights and replacing them yearly for fear of leaks. It's wondering if the house needs repainting and quickly squashing that thought. It's taking appliances to be repaired and picking them up when they're fixed. It's keeping an eye on the freezer so that it stays my friend and doesn't, back turned, become my enemy. It's vacuuming dog hair and sand from the car in a regular sort of way. It's inviting friends for dinner because sitting around the table is a good way to stay in touch. It's making plans for summer holidays. And it's so much more.

These days, once my apron is off and the weekend comes around, I am free to do things that I enjoy doing at home – renovating, cooking, sewing, music, drawing and gardening. Doing these things draws me out of myself, beyond my daily busyness and my ego's determination to get things done. They give back in surprising ways. When I pick up a pair of secateurs and head into the garden, I stop fighting whatever it is that I spend so much of my mental life wrestling with. By the time I come back in, after soaking up the natural beauty all around me, I feel at one with time passing. Spending time in the garden gives me valuable breathing space, away from my family and work, to get on with just being me.

It's not that I stop caring about family and work when I'm cutting back ivy or making bread. I don't. It's more that these activities are on another level. Crunching scissors into fabric, slapping dough on a bench and spying seedlings poking up through the soil – these feel deeply satisfying. Soulful, even. Lying in bed on Sunday night, thinking back on my day, it's making pastry and winding bean tendrils around a stake that flash through my mind. While I'll never be expert at baking or gardening, just tackling them gives me a buoyancy – a holiday from myself – which keeps bringing me back to them.

Now that my kids are older, and we live in Hobart, many of my deepest pleasures are found at home. I love slipping into a freshly-made bed with line-dried sheets. I relish sipping tea with a friend at the kitchen table. I get excited about choosing fabric for a sewing project. And I'm always looking for an excuse to visit the plant nursery. These things return me to childhood joys. But they also usher in a contentment that's hard to find words for. They are simple things. Not even that interesting to relate. And yet none of them are easy things. They don't happen naturally. They assume time, energy, imagination and love. Are they consolations from my efforts to balance work and family? Perhaps. What I do know is that whenever I'm feeling overwhelmed, and my heart shrinks just a little, gardening and playing the piano are the first things to disappear from my day, however much I miss them when they do.

I'm not advocating a return to the 50s housewife, with her polished floors and subordination to the needs of her family. I'm keen to find satisfaction at home. But I'm also alive to the tentacle-like pull of household demands. While being at home offers me creative freedom away from the public eye, it too easily slips into a spiral of thankless chores. Like the sorcerer's apprentice, with too few mops and buckets to halt the flooding basement steps, in the wrong mood home work has a way of turning into the trap we call housework.

Housework has a bad reputation, and rightly so. For nearly everyone I know, it's a source of stress and frustration. It frustrates me too. Except it isn't just frustration that I feel when I do it. After pulling on my apron, and getting on with what needs doing, I nearly always take off my apron feeling better about myself and my place in the world than when I put it on.

I'm not alone in having mixed feelings for the home, in my push-pull relationship to it. I think this is because home work takes in so much. Staying on top of my home's day-to-day running, creating and sustaining attractive living spaces, cleaning up after myself and my family, cooking in a nurturing way, and sustaining the love that makes all this worthwhile – these are very different activities. Could this explain the heated confusion that tends to arise whenever domesticity does come up in conversation?

A few years ago, at the end of a phone call with my mother from her nursing home in Adelaide to my kitchen in Hobart, she asked me a question that stopped me in my tracks. 'Do you think', she asked, 'that I've wasted my life?' Thinking I'd misheard her – she'd always staunchly defended the value of home – I asked her to repeat her question. She did so, this time with more insistence. 'Course not', I replied, feeling offended on her behalf, and listed her accomplishments as they streamed through my mind – running a busy home, farming, charity work, gardening, various sports and a close circle of friends.

Yet my mother's question stayed with me. In the weeks and months that followed, I kept circling back to it. Because what I heard my mother ask, through the echo chamber of our relationship, was whether she'd wasted her life at home. She hadn't wasted her life, I told myself. Or had she?

Fifteen years after my husband and I started a family, I decided it was time that I understood my relationship to home better. I didn't just want to understand it better, I needed to understand it. Big questions that had haunted me since my early 20s, caught up with me and became pressing. Was there, I wanted to know, an art to keeping a home? And if so, what was it? Was it possible to find meaning and satisfaction in housekeeping? And did this have something important to teach us about life itself? Eventually these questions snowballed into one giant question. *Was our home work essential to living a good life or did it take away from it?*

I began by reading everything I could find on the subject. This proved so fascinating that it took me a while to realise that my research wasn't addressing what was really an existential question about the value of my devotion to family and home. So I did an about-turn. Instead of fossicking in the library, or burrowing on-line, I would use my own experience of home work to answer my questions. I would be scientist and student. I wouldn't don a white coat. But I would tell the story of my unfolding relationship to home, from watching my mother around the house as a girl, to clearing up after my family in a home that I once dreamed of and ended up running single-handed. And in telling this story, I would find out whether an attractive home was indeed worth the effort that running it demanded.

For all my questions, whenever I put away my phone and dived into something creative at home, I enjoyed myself. I loved smelling a slow-cooked casserole fill the house in winter. I felt like the girl I once was on coming into the kitchen with tomatoes from the garden warming each hand. I got a special kind of pride from sewing a duvet cover with fabric that meant something to me, that had a history. I might struggle to credit these things as valuable, in the eyes of the world, but they always brought me joy.

In a way, everything that follows is my response to my mother's question about whether she wasted her life at home. Because it's not just her question. Ultimately, to the degree that we value looking after ourselves, our home and the people we love most, it's everyone's question. And this story is my answer to it.

1. childhood things

'I can't be really creative until I have a clear horizon
and all the road is clear ahead – then I can be as happy as can be'.
Alfred Hitchcock

When I was little, the game I liked best was hide and seek. My favourite
hiding place was in the linen cupboard at the top of the stairs, so wide and
generous that its door was the width of a normal door. Inside were shelves
stacked high with sheets, towels and blankets. Beneath each stack was a
label: 'single', coloured stripy sheets for us girls, 'double', white sheets for
Mum and Dad, and for 'guests', special white sheets. I barely noticed this
impressive organisational system. The fact that our house was well-ordered
was neither here nor there to me, it just was.

It was the bottom of the linen cupboard that I loved. Just big enough
for one of my sisters or me – whoever got there first – to climb into, all
summer long it was stacked with feather-filled eiderdowns. The door to
the cupboard had a catch that could be pulled shut and opened from the
inside, making this padded cave a perfect hiding place. A vertical chink
of light came through the gap at the edge of the door, and there was a
slight smell of mothballs. With the worn cotton covers against my skin,
the plush of down beneath, I could have stayed there forever.

I was a teenager before I noticed that my mother was always in a rush, so
natural was it to me that she would be. She was doing flowers for a church
wedding. She was taking one of my sisters to the dentist. She was cutting
sandwiches for school lunches. Or she was volunteering for a charity event.
Bristling with energy as she moved about the house, she was brushing
away cobwebs, planting out tomatoes or beating cream and vanilla to top
meringues. 'How does she do it?' her friends asked each other, impressed

by Mum's ability to get things done. Increasingly, I asked myself, '*Why does she do it?*' Mum was the centre of our family's world, the reason the train of our lives ran on time. Yet the taller I grew, the more mysterious her life seemed to me.

It didn't strike me as a very interesting mystery. I didn't need to know more about Mum's life than the ripples it made on my own, because I never imagined my life following hers. I kept my big questions for my father, whose answers I hung on or challenged, depending on my mood. Dad was my north star and guide. He couldn't make apple cake or ratatouille to save himself, but he was open to my stream of whys. He didn't always have an answer, but he always heard me out, and this was enough to keep me coming back with more questions.

Dad was the most solid thing in my life, which is why I felt daunted by the query hanging over him after his first heart attack in my early teens. He made it clear to me that he may not be around forever. I can only begin to imagine what it must have been like for Mum to have four teenage daughters and a husband with heart problems under one roof. At the time, merciless and acne-prone, I didn't even try. I just assumed that, for reasons of her own, she flew into tempers. And while I didn't like her temper, over time I found ways to manage it – mainly by keeping out of her way until she calmed down. I never feared I might inherit her temper because, again, I wasn't planning to follow in her footsteps. I would never use heavy hand-cream, warm up chicken mornay, play championship golf, book regular hair appointments, wear court shoes or develop bunions – of these things I was sure.

After leaving school and starting an Arts degree, I continued to live at home. Turning inward, I was at times unreachable. Sitting on a wood-box by the front door, in a creeping patch of sunlight, I'd lose myself in a novel for the next day's seminar. Out of the corner of my eye, I'd spy Mum on the stairs, her arms full of folded laundry. Mostly I ignored Mum's housekeeping. But I was increasingly conscious of our cleaning woman, Mrs Bryce. The matter-of-fact way Mrs Bryce cleaned our house every Monday morning made me feel awkward, out of place. Shouldn't I be doing something more useful with my time than burying myself in a book? Reading, writing and riding my bike were all very well. But they weren't solid and real, like emptying the bins and vacuuming the stairs. I understood, from eyeing Mrs Bryce at a distance, that housekeeping was no small thing.

Mrs Bryce sucked musk sweets as she dusted, leaving her wicker basket with polish, cloths and cleaning spray at the door of each room. Next, she vacuumed the floors, pushing our heavy upright around the house until the carpet pile lay in thick stripes and the timber furniture shone. Mrs Bryce had a way of turning what looked like a chore to me into work that she seemed proud of. Mid-morning, she put down her basket, filled the kettle and had tea with Mum, assuming she was at home. If I was in earshot, I might overhear them asking after each other's husbands. Next Mrs Bryce would report on her grandson who'd just started walking. 'And what about those curtains in the living room', Mum would ask. 'Couldn't they do with a clean?' These were hardly world-shattering events, I thought to myself as I passed through the kitchen on my way out the back door. They weren't important matters. They were details that even George Eliot and Charles Dickens didn't stoop to in their novels. And neither, I vowed, would I.

Often, when Mrs Bryce arrived and changed into the slippers that she chose to work in, Mum disappeared out the back door. She was off to have her hair done. She was late for a charity meeting. She was lifting buckets of flowers into the boot of the car for a church wedding. She was scrambling to find car keys before a golf match. But for most of the week, Mum was busy round the house: unpacking the dishwasher; peeling vegetables; deadheading roses; icing a cake; ordering groceries; sorting laundry; or darning socks. I wasn't ungrateful. And I always did what she asked me to do around the house. I just didn't offer to help her.

The work that Mum did seemed dull to me. Still, I loved everything about our house in a way that felt so natural as to be unconscious. I loved it for some of the things that Mum didn't like about it – a garden big enough to lose myself in, floorboards that squeaked on every third step, and a dark kitchen that Mum had wallpapered in a run of breezy prints but was never able to renovate. She loved our house too. But for her it was a long way from the laundry downstairs to the linen cupboard upstairs. Each spring, her back ached from shoveling compost onto garden beds on three sides of the house. And while I never noticed the chairs in our living room getting shabby, I did notice how the room came alive when the chairs were re-covered in a bold print. And only much later did I realise that all the while I remained oblivious of my home's soft furnishings, playing behind the sofa rather than chatting demurely on it, I was building up an imaginative relationship to my every future home.

One day, on a visit to a junk shop with Mum, I found an iron bedstead which I persuaded her to buy for me. After painting the metal frame in cream enamel and assembling it in my bedroom, I asked if I might dye my pink blankets navy. Navy blankets were striking, pink blankets were not. Then it was the pictures on the walls that needed changing, from watercolours of landscapes to modernist prints. I was looking for something in my bedroom, a boldness and daring that I was searching for in myself. Drawing, crafting and repurposing things were deep and private pleasures. Changing my bedroom was my first shot at changing my surroundings. Waking up in a cream metal double bed, under navy blankets, was surprisingly rewarding.

This discovery unnerved me. I'd been educated to think that things were worth doing to the degree that they bolstered my CV and drew social credit, and not for the satisfaction they gave in the moment. Shouldn't I be more interested in world politics and the arc of my career than in sanding back furniture and losing myself in a drawing? There was nothing wrong, in principle, with cooking and drawing and growing plants from seed. They were just less important than building a career, travelling to far-flung places and having a five-year plan. Yet most days, after classes at university, I'd hop off my bike, head upstairs and flop on my bed, finding sanctuary from the rush of university life in the clean lines of my bedroom.

In my third year of university, I moved into a share house on the other side of town. Three months later, my father died from a heart attack. Shortly after that my mother sold our family house, and she and I moved into a Victorian two-bedroom bluestone. (My sisters had moved out of home before me, which made me the logical one to keep Mum company.) Finally I had a bedroom with bare floorboards. Except, of course, the patina of family life was gone. And so, on weekends, Mum and I would coax the dog into the back of the car and drive to the beach house where Dad, in spirit, still was. I found it comforting to imagine him on the balcony and at the head of the kitchen table. Except that I could only see him in my mind's eye, as in a daydream. And daydreams, I realised, don't last.

Before dinner, I'd carry the standing lamp from the living room into the kitchen and plug it in next to the table, to soften things that way. I couldn't change what had happened. I couldn't bring Dad back. But I could soften the light in the kitchen when Mum and I sat down to eat. Yet both of us knew that we couldn't spend weekends at the beach forever. The world as we'd known it had ended. We no longer had an upstairs linen cupboard. Mum accepted this more easily than I did, and her acceptance made it easier for me to follow suit. Family and home were the two constants that I'd taken for granted, and I was ready to let them go. It was time to start afresh, to create my own sense of home somewhere else. And so, on finishing my degree, I made an important move.

2. flat-sharing, life-sharing

'You can learn as much – or more – from one glance at a private space
as you can from hours of exposure to a public space'.
Malcolm Gladwell, *Blink*

The morning I arrived in London, and moved into a share flat, I met my
English roommate for the first time. Luckily both of us came from big
families and had shared flats before. On my second day in the city, I got
a job in a health food restaurant, making it easy to make friends, eat well,
get my bearings and pay the rent.

I had arrived and, for the first few months, this was enough. Even ordinary things like shopping and commuting felt exciting for being undertaken
in a teeming metropolis. Except that this was no BBC television series of
the kind I watched in my parents' bedroom as a teenager, eating smug-
gled in biscuits when I should have been doing school assignments. Nor
was I a character in a novel by Martin Amis or AS Byatt. This was the
next chapter of my life.

It was the mid-80s. There was no Skype and phone calls were expensive. For much of the time, I was on my own. I didn't mind. I felt guided
by something deeper than intent, bigger than any goal. It was a desire to
discover what life might offer if I pushed its boundaries. After a sheltered
childhood, it was exhilarating to be making my own way in the world, to
be accountable to life itself and not to my family or education.

A year later, when my share flat was put on the market, the need to make
plans arose. My time in London had gone beyond a working holiday. Now
I was there to live. I had no strategy, but I trusted people, as they seemed
to trust me. My first and longest-running flat was with a girl in marketing who was engaged to a naval officer. When she married, I extended

the flat's lease with two guys I met after I put an ad in the evening paper. Compared to Australian standards, our flat in South London was a shoebox, especially when friends stayed over. Yet for three rich years it was home.

Friends and boyfriends came and went. But my pine desk, wicker armchair, pink eiderdown and framed pictures came with me wherever I happened to be living. Simply having them in my room made that space feel like home – not easy when home was a dark basement flat on a short lease, or a family house-sit for friends.

During my nine lives in London, first south and then north of the river, I became very sensitive to living spaces. I wasn't concerned with decoration so much as atmosphere, which I picked up on the moment I entered a new space, whether it was an open-plan office, a homely kitchen or a tiny courtyard. All the intangibles that bring a space to life became like a second language to me.

Every few years, my mother would fly out to visit me. Once her jetlag subsided, she'd do a quick inventory of my life, cautiously admiring whatever I was up to. But she never really understood why I stayed on in London. Why, she would come close to asking, was I living in a cramped flat, working long hours teaching English to foreign students – a job that might not lead to anything?

The question I'd left Adelaide to escape, what to do with my life, had followed me shadow-like to London. I still didn't have an answer. However, the longer I lived overseas, the more convinced I became that work was what you did for pay in an office. It meant peer reviews and a graded salary. It didn't involve volunteer and charity work, which made up the bulk of Mum's work in Adelaide. Despite our good intentions, Mum and I struggled to see the value of each other's choices, to the point that I felt relieved to see her off at the end of her stay. After taking the Tube home from the airport and jiggling my key in the lock, for a split second I saw my flat through her eyes, as poky and lacking in outdoor space. But as soon as I passed through the living room the critical voice in my head fell quiet. And, by the time I'd made myself a cup of tea, I was in love with our cosy flat all over again.

For the first five years I lived in London, I shared a string of flats and focused on my career. Staying on top of housekeeping was no big deal. I could fit everything in after work or on the weekend. Every day I gave over a bit of time to cooking, organising, errands and shopping. This involved imagination and effort. However something in me refused to see the value of my efforts at home. I made sure that the place where I lived was pleasant and comfortable, but I made little of it. Like everyone I knew, I moaned about the washing up, despaired of long to-do lists, and avoided opening certain cupboards in the company of friends. Like my friends, I found it easier to complain of all the jobs piled up at home than to describe the little joys I'd discovered there. I was more likely to tell a friend about how messy my flat was than to describe the spells of harmony that I found immersed in drawing, or reading a book.

One weekend, a girlfriend asked me to join her on a visit to her aunt who had retired to the country. Ann had no children. No partner complicated her life. She lived in a house with a rolling garden in the middle of Norfolk farm land. Even so, within minutes of our arrival, I saw there was nothing retiring about Julie's aunt. She was strikingly self-possessed, her greying hair pulled back off her face. Rain or shine, Ann worked in her garden. On top of the fridge in the kitchen sat a stack of gardening diaries, filled with plantings, prunings and moving of beds. In the pantry, jars of home-made jam, preserves and pickles lined the shelves. Near the front door was a shed devoted to the hardening off of plants in row on row of pots. The downstairs bathroom was set up with a scrubbing brush, gritty soap, hand cream and a rack for upturned boots. Ann's house felt lived in and loved.

Whenever Ann had summer visitors, like her niece and me, she cooked big meals, serving lunch beneath the blousy branches of a copper ash. Then, after waving her visitors off, she went back to eating scrambled eggs on her knee in front of the evening news, with an early alarm for the next morning. Ann's life was singular. She was doing what she loved and was doing it well. While it was clear that fortune had been kind to her, her grit and staying power came from within. When Julie and I arrived, I was skeptical of Ann's way of life. But by the time she dropped us off at the train station on Sunday night, I felt only admiration for her.

That Christmas, I didn't renew my contract for another year of language teaching. I still thank this experience for bringing me out of my shell and into contact with scores of people I'd otherwise never have known. It gave me huge respect for the bravery of people who pack up homes that they may never return to in the hope of a better life elsewhere. Still, my mother was right, teaching English to foreign students wasn't something that I wanted to do forever. And so, after enrolling in a fast-track secretarial course, with a view to entering publishing, I taught my last class and left.

On first meeting Susie in class, I thought her a bit haughty. Tall and slender, her brown hair cut in a way that freed her curls, she didn't look like a secretarial student. This wasn't just because she'd made her own clothes as a fashion student. Nor was it that she was above learning shorthand. As it was for me, gaining secretarial skills was a way for her to break into a new industry. For her, it was a door into design work. For me, it was into the world of books.

During breaks from our course, Susie drank lemon tea and nibbled almonds – not a snack that I'd thought of having in my handbag. Before long, we were having tea together most mornings, groaning about our low shorthand and typing speeds as other students hit over a 100 words a minute, to our plodding 40.

In the coming months, I spent weekends with Susie at her mother's home in Norwich, a three-hour train ride from London. Louise, Susie's mother, gave me her son's old bedroom, with its blanket-lined curtains against the cold and well-stocked bookcase. At breakfast, she talked up the benefits of wheatgerm on muesli and made tea with a mixture of leaves in the pot. She soaked legumes overnight, took a wicker basket to the Farmer's Market, had meals at fixed times, and expressed a keen interest in politics. Her modest semi-detached house, with its lovingly tended narrow garden, contrasted with Ann's large house and garden. Yet the hospitality these women extended to me, a young Australian in London, stemmed from the same root. It was love and generosity and I appreciated it hugely.

I was by now accustomed to forging a path in London. I'd forgotten how nice it felt to be looked after by someone who really cared about me. It was relaxing not to have to think about the scores of things that keep a home ticking over, from buying groceries, to keeping a fire alight, to making enough soup for lunch the next day. Most of all, I'd forgotten what it feels like to be loved in a family setting, where it was as natural to be offered advice on a housing issue as to share stories from my personal life. Sitting on the train on Sunday night, wondering if my flatmates would be up when I got home, I felt a little leap of sadness as I braced myself for the working week ahead.

I did eventually manage a respectable typing speed and was soon working as a temp for the Marketing Manager of *Vogue* magazine. One morning, when I should have been filing my boss's tax receipts, an advertisement for 'The *Vogue* Young Talent Competition' caught my eye. Entrants were asked to write an opinion piece, a story, and to interview someone of interest. I arranged to interview the director of a publishing house with offices tucked behind Trafalgar Square. Carmen Callil, who founded Virago Press for out-of-print women authors from her kitchen table, now had the corner office at Chatto & Windus. From the moment I asked my first question, Carmen made it clear that her time was precious and that she was doing me a favour in agreeing to the interview. Carmen was Australian, which explained her directness and quite possibly her willingness to speak with me. I knew my chances of winning the contest were slim. However when, at the end of our hour together, she offered me a job in publicity – she wasn't wasting her time after all – I agreed straight away.

In marketing meetings, Carmen had no patience for anyone around the table who wasn't prepared. She made frequent complaints about badly-worded minutes from prior meetings, which made me relieved that it wasn't my job to take them. Until one afternoon, six months into my career in publicity, Carmen lost her temper and fired her Personal Assistant for some minor misdemeanor. The following Monday, I was moved into the office next to hers to take over the vacancy.

Susie and her mother were a constant support during this period. We went on rugged upcountry walks and ate hearty stews in front of the fire. I was still living in my small share flat south of the Thames, and dating an articled lawyer in a half-hearted way. More and more, I looked forward to long weekends with Susie and Louise, a hundred miles north of work deadlines, lunch eaten at my desk and dark walks home from the Tube.

I grew to love Louise. She was the kind of mother I didn't have. Partly, of course, because she wasn't my mother. Louise was good at supporting me because she believed in me and the woman I was trying to become. She was able to guide me, nudge me, because she understood me in a way that made me want to live up to her belief in me. Importantly, my relationship to Louise wasn't tempered, as with my own mother, by criticism. And the openness that this encouraged created an atmosphere in which I felt able to unfurl and give deeply of myself.

In the end it was my bad minute-taking in meetings that lost me the job. A year and a half into the role, Carmen gave me a dark look, called me into her office, poured us both a whisky in thick-bottomed glasses, and fired me. 'You know', she said, sighing, 'you're like a princess in a tower. And it's time you came down and worked out what you're going to do with your life.' Sounding more like an exasperated friend than an employer, I knew her intentions were good. Her words hurt. But there was truth in them. I didn't know what I wanted from a career in publishing. I only knew that I loved dealing with words and with people's innermost thoughts. I was ambitious to get on in publishing. But there was no particular role that I was pining for, angling for. All the same, being Carmen's assistant wasn't a good fit. She was right about that. 'Take a walk round the block', Carmen said, ushering me out. 'And come back and tell me what kind of reference you want me to write.'

I could have returned to Australia at that point. But it never entered my head. Instead I enrolled in postgraduate study. As it happened, studying literature turned out to be a mistake. It was too close to my undergraduate degree. Still, it gave me courage to start a Ph.D. close to my heart, in psychology and literature. This gave me permission to spend days on end reading Sigmund Freud and other psychologists in The British Library, with visits to my supervisor in Oxford. I also branched out as a volunteer, manning the phone at The Women's Therapy Centre. And I became an observer in a mental health team in East London, to see where all this might lead me.

The women who called up the therapy centre, to enquire about counselling, rarely mentioned their relationship or sexual problems, as reading Sigmund Freud had led me to expect they might. Obviously there was more to their stories than they were willing to confide over the phone. Even so, their problems seemed existential, stemming from the sheer difficulty of life. Often I heard small children scampering around in the background, which confirmed to me that family life tends to complicate rather than simplify a woman's life.

At night, I looked forward to taking the bus home to my share flat, after studying in the library or working Saturdays in a bookshop. Staring out the bus window, I daydreamed about having my own place, and what that might be like. Still, my mind was made up that domestic life didn't matter. It was a sideline and not the main thing. The more liberated I became, and the longer I ducked thoughts about having a family and its unappealingly titled home duties, the more a subtle form of chauvinism coloured my attitude to the home. Women who took pride in running a home – baking cakes and running up curtains – were consoling themselves. They were making themselves feel better about a life which subordinated their desires to their family's needs, to a life without power or a room of their own.

I was full of contradictions. I kept up my love of gardens by visiting them whenever I got the chance. I got dirt under my nails planting herbs in a window box. And I avoided cooking, even while I fantasised about being a good cook. I never imagined that returning the gleam to the kitchen, after dinner with friends, would one day give me a flash of pride. Or that picking flowers for the windowsill, and braising meat for a casserole, could ever come to feel like achievements. The dishes got done and the bedlinen got changed but my eyes stayed trained on the horizon.

And yet, and yet. I'd never have lived in London for as long as I did, had I not enjoyed the generosity of a host of people I met along the way. Without their willingness to include me in their dinners, weekends away, holidays and special occasions my life would have been far less rich and a whole lot lonelier. Growing up, I'd taken my mother's hospitality for granted, to the point of dismissing her efforts. But by this point in my life, I felt grateful when a friend brought around soup when I fell sick, or sent me an invitation at Christmas. Sandwiches on a hike, a present on my birthday, things like these touched my heart and made me want to extend my own kindness; a loaf of soda bread, a home-made pie, to others. I struggled to return these gestures from my small share flat. However I vowed that one day I'd repay them in kind. And so even while my thoughts were focused on my career, in my heart – a place I didn't often go – I never doubted that there was an art to running a home and that it was a worthwhile thing to do.

CB

There are two ways to tell the story of my awakening to the power of home. The conventional story, told from the outside, is that I grew up in a family of four girls and enjoyed a sheltered childhood in Adelaide. After university, following my father's death, I ventured overseas to expand my horizons and follow my own path. Over eighteen years in London, I taught English to foreign students, switched into publishing and then into post-graduate education before eventually training as a psychotherapist. Five years into my time in the UK, I met the man who, seven years later, I would marry and start a family with, all the while keeping a foot in the door of my career.

However there is another way to tell this story; from inside the cupboard at the top of the stairs of my childhood home, where I once hid among the eiderdowns, the polished cotton covers soft against my skin. I was completely at home there, with just enough light to feel cocooned but not trapped. I even loved the smell of mothballs from the stacks of linen above. And while I could have stayed there forever, I liked knowing that one of my sisters was about to open the door and spring me from my hiding place.

The official story is that we grow up, leave home, become independent, or at least transfer our dependencies onto new relationships. This is an easy story to tell, it rolls off the tongue in a comfortable third-person, past tense. However growing up wasn't like this for me. The reality was that I struggled to separate from my family, even after my father died. The process didn't feel a bit natural to me. I found looking after myself hard. It wasn't independence that I lacked. I was possibly more independent than many of my friends. And I knew how to get on in the world. My real dilemma took place inside myself, in my struggle to feel that I was worth looking after. And so, unable to confront this straight on, five years into my time in London, I applied for postgraduate study and entered my own therapy.

Being in therapy gave me a feel for my experience from the inside. I went into therapy because I needed help standing on my own feet. However, as one thing led to another, I got curious about other things too. Being in therapy allowed me to explore my inner world in the company of someone who could accompany me there without holding my hand. Through it I was able to find out what I found satisfying, for some people finding it is utterly simple but not for me. Thanks to it – and this felt enormous – I came to appreciate the value of things and not just their cost. I came to feel wholehearted about life, rather than confused and defensive. Being in therapy wasn't a magical wand. But I did feel stronger, less buffeted by life. I got better at making decisions and felt less emotionally reactive – particularly towards my mother, whose shortcomings I came to forgive and strengths to respect.

After five years of flatsharing, north and south of the Thames, moving into a studio flat felt like a watershed. Living alone, while being in therapy, gave me space to discover that there was nothing I needed to escape from, that I had what it took to look after myself, and that my strengths and weaknesses issued from the same source. Not being accountable to anyone else helped me to see that I didn't need permission to express myself creatively. At times it felt lonely, living on my own. But these spells were outweighed by long periods of calm in which I felt as emotionally at home as I had in the eiderdown cupboard as a girl. Knowing that I could return to my little bolt-hole, at the end of the day, gave me strength to look inside rather than outside myself for reassurance, and for satisfaction in my choices.

My studio flat was different from previous places that I'd lived, possibly because I door-knocked to find it. Brian, who owned the house, was a television producer who travelled for work and let out the ground floor so that the house looked inhabited when he was away. As soon as I moved in, I saw that our tastes were wildly different. The only furniture in my ground-floor studio was a wooden double bed, around the top of which an electric train ran on metal tracks, long since broken – a present from one of Brian's arty friends. One wall of the bedroom had floor to ceiling sheet-metal cupboards. The tiny bathroom was lined with black vinyl with naked bulbs around the mirror, with a toilet opening on to a garage that housed an old Land Rover. Brian's part of the house upstairs, which he rarely cleaned, brimmed with primary colours, bean bags and hip artworks.

Living in a studio, with daily chats to Brian, felt like the best of both worlds. He encouraged me to decorate the studio as I pleased. After painting the walls white, I threw a cream bedspread over the bright purple sofa, planted herbs in the tiniest garden and made bookcases from stacked wooden crates. I listened to my own music and drew when I felt like it at weekends. Losing myself in a novel, sitting between chimney pots on the roof, felt continuous with the freedom I'd found between the covers of books as a teenager. During the day, I was back studying literature, apprenticed to learning once more. Having my own place, with friends nearby, suited me well.

I soon worked out that if I wanted clean lines in my studio, it was up to me to keep it that way. No more sharing household tasks with unwilling flatmates. No more lopsided rosters. There was just my own reluctance to deal with. I soon worked out that it was easier to overcome my resistance to housekeeping by setting aside Saturday mornings to clean, shop and do laundry, than it was to do these tasks in bits during the week. I didn't love cleaning. Yet as soon as I got on with it, my energy shifted from 'No I won't' to 'Yes I can'. And, when I was done, I felt a real sense of accomplishment as I sat with a cup of tea in a clean and tranquil space.

3. settling

Paul declared, early on, his wish to move in with me. We couldn't, he said, be in a serious relationship and not live together. This was news to me. Previous to meeting Paul, I'd been happy to keep my relationships casual. They were important but never the main thing. But Paul, a few years younger, crept behind my defences and got me to love him in a deeper way. Even so, it took a lot of persuading to convince me that I wanted to share my flat, even with him. I'd worked hard for my independence, finding ways to enjoy and not just endure my solitude. But Paul persisted and within a few months my studio flat became our studio flat.

Paul and I quickly came to an understanding about what matters most in life. We read each other's books, went for long walks, cooked Italian food and were drawn to the same European cities. We weren't ideally suited. He thought nothing of teaching himself Greek and reading James Joyce's *Ulysses,* both of which were beyond me. Still, these felt like minor details which didn't cloud the overall picture of our relationship.

There was, however, one big difference. Paul had left home on a scholarship at 17, moving straight into a university college. Could this explain why he downplayed the effort that a well-run flat required? All the same, from the day Paul moved in, he understood that my need for order and beauty was greater than my dislike of housekeeping. And while he didn't share this view, he accepted it – and that was enough for me.

When Paul and I met, he was straight out of university. The fact that I was older meant I'd got the hang of looking after myself before we got together. Not only had I the hang of it, I was proud of being able to do so. I still didn't want to be a homemaker, but I did feel that housekeeping was worth the effort. I loved waking up in my own clean space and returning to a smoothly-run home. I liked getting the housework over with on Saturday mornings and shopping with a list on my way home from work. I was pretty good at doing household tasks I didn't relish and I liked knowing what was in the fridge. I accepted that there is no such thing as later and that putting off tasks doesn't make them any easier. I knew that housework takes fifty percent longer than I usually allowed for it and that having a fixed day to change the bedlinen suited me better than waiting until I was in the mood to do it. On balance, I was pretty good at caring about household tasks that I didn't ultimately care about. And these were lessons that, learned the hard way, proved impossible to forget.

Paul had trained in politics and philosophy. There wasn't a verbal argument that he couldn't win. As my hot-headed mother's daughter, I was reluctant to lose my temper over small things. And yet domestic life is made up of countless small things which, added together, join up to become one very big thing. Paul, for his part, didn't see it this way. He liked having herbs on the windowsill and a clean kitchen, well enough. But perhaps because he'd never had to roll up his sleeves and fight for them, they weren't part of who he felt he was.

In some ways, my domestic competence, my desire to keep our flat ship-shape, worked against me. Sensing how much I hated nagging, Paul hung back until I picked up the slack. Clearly he was lucky to live with someone for whom housekeeping was second nature, who tackled tasks as they arose. Paul always cooked when friends came for dinner, but otherwise I did most of what needed doing round the flat. Still, our relationship cut both ways. There is more to life than housekeeping, and I felt lucky to be with someone who was interested in my emotional and professional life, who listened patiently for however long it took for me to come to terms with my sticky thoughts and feelings. I hadn't had this with anyone since my father died, and it felt precious to me.

Nine months after Paul moved in, my landlord made it clear that Paul was one person too many in his house. Within the month, Paul and I had moved into a one-bedroom flat in North London and the next chapter of my life, our life, began. Our flat was near the unfashionable corner of Hampstead Heath and a walkable distance to the university I was teaching at. The faded pink eiderdown, which had lain on my bed during seven moves across London, finally had a permanent home.

Moving into a flat with Paul freed up my thinking. For the first time since arriving in London, I was able to see more than a few steps ahead in my career. Much as I liked teaching literature, I didn't want to spend the rest of my days presenting research papers at conferences. Presenting weekly seminars that teased out the meaning of chunky novels was stressful. And it was a strain to teach literary theories – Adorno, Foucault, Derrida – that I could barely follow myself. I felt more comfortable in my office, talking to students one-to-one about their essays and personal circumstances than I ever did at the front of a lecture theatre. Moving into a flat with Paul opened me up to a bigger canvas. What was the point of mugging up on tricky philosophical theories, when what I liked most was helping students to do their best work? Perhaps, I thought, I could be of more use to others in a therapeutic setting.

Manning the advice phoneline at The Women's Therapy Centre gave me a taste of what this might be like. I found myself wanting more of it. I was tired of reading books. I wanted to drop a bucket into the well of life and drink from its source. Working as a counsellor gave me a taste for the kind of intimacy that springs up when two people are alone in a room without an agenda. Perhaps, by training as a therapist, I could help others while pursuing my own interests. This became my plan. I would keep on teaching, before moving sideways to train as a psychotherapist. Finally I had a five-year plan. I knew what I wanted and was in a position to go after it.

CB

I was hitting my stride professionally, when my therapist fell pregnant for a second time. Some mornings, arriving for an early session, I could hear her toddler playing upstairs. Watching my therapist's belly grow triggered fantasises about what pregnancy might be like for me. Paul and I had been together for five years. Vague background thoughts about marriage had turned into plans to marry. Everything that my independent life had safely sidelined came crowding in. Could I imagine being married? Did I secretly want a baby? Was my relationship to Paul strong enough, solid enough, for us to build a family on?

I was changing the bedlinen, one Saturday morning, and Paul was chomping at the bit to walk into town with me.

'Can't you just wait while I get these sheets into the machine?' I asked him.

'Sure', he said, and disappeared from the bedroom. A few minutes later, he returned. 'Ready?'

'Just about', I said, slipping on a pillow case.

'Couldn't you do that later? It's noon, late already.'

I sighed.

'Why?' asked Paul, annoyed by my sigh, 'do you have to do everything just so? What does it matter if the sheets are washed now or later?'

'Well', I said, 'if I wash them now, I can dry them on the balcony and save on the drier.'

'But', he said, 'who cares about the power bill when we're always late for everything? Why don't you just admit that you're so small-minded that the outside world doesn't really exist for you?'

In the scheme of things, being called small-minded was fairly tame. All the same, I felt insulted. Paul, it seemed, saw me as inward looking, lacking in culture and preoccupied with trivial, domestic things. Lifting the mattress to tuck in a sheet, I decided, in that split second, that I didn't want to be anyone's wife. Not because I didn't love Paul, I did. I just didn't trust myself not to care about all the wrong things once I was married – the conventional, little things that would distract me from a big-hearted, ambitious life.

Paul was right about my love of the domestic. I made no secret of admiring people with smoothly-running homes. When friends came for dinner, I did the washing up before going to bed. I scanned the household tips section of magazines with the same zeal that my trader cousin checked share prices. Much as I hated to admit it, little household things like a broken vacuum cleaner, or an issue with a neighbour, had a way of becoming big and powerful in my mind.

When I picked up Simone de Beauvoir's *The Second Sex*, it fell open at a section that confirmed my every misgiving about the pitfalls of domesticity. 'Washing, ironing, sweeping out fluff from under wardrobes – all this halting of decay', de Beauvoir wrote, 'is also the denial of life; for time simultaneously creates and destroys, and only its negative aspect concerns the housekeeper.' It was hard enough keeping my life afloat in its present incarnation. What if I had a family and was reduced to spending my days ferreting out fluff from under wardrobes?

The next morning, I called off our wedding. To my surprise, nothing happened. The sky didn't fall in. My mother cancelled her flight to London, Paul and I went on living together, I continued to see my therapist, and I felt hugely relieved that I wasn't about to become anyone's wife.

Two months later, on holiday in France on the honeymoon we'd already paid for, Paul and I met up with my mother and a friend of hers in the hillside town of Uzes. Suzanne led gardening tours, and she and Mum were checking out gardens in the surrounding countryside. It was a hot night and, after the four of us caught up over dinner, Paul and I returned to our room where he promptly stretched out on the bed with a volume of Proust. Too hot to sleep, I took a cup of mint tea on to the roof, where the air was cool and my thoughts could roam.

As I stared up at the sky, I heard women's voices. It took a minute to realise that Mum's was one of them. Her voice sounded softer and more sing-song than the one that had carried me through childhood. A bottle chinked against ice and two plumes of smoke rose into the sky. Mum sounded happy. No longer housekeeping for a family of six, her voice was light, playful even. Released from baskets of laundry and trips into town for new school shoes, her voice floated above the rooftops.

When Mum and Suzanne retired, I stayed on, sitting cross-legged on the roof. It wasn't the prospect of having a child, I realised, that I felt wary of. It was the housekeeping that accompanied family life that bothered me. It was those unappealingly titled home duties that I didn't have an answer to. I didn't want to end up a dirt-avenging housekeeper, brandishing her chores like a sword to ward off the meaninglessness of her existence. Sitting on the hotel roof, my thinking on this felt as clear as the stars in the sky.

Even without a child in the mix, more household tasks fell to me than to my Proust-reading partner, simply because my resistance to doing them was lower than his. If we went on to have a baby together, wasn't I risking spending a big chunk of my life caring about a raft of domestic things that nearly everyone I knew considered trivial? Even I thought them trivial. Yet their pull on me was undeniable. I envied people, like Paul's mother, who routinely left the dishes in the sink because, in her words, 'God doesn't mind dirty dishes.'

Sitting up late in that small French town there seemed reason to worry. What to do? If I was to move through this logjam, I needed to understand the push and pull that it triggered in me. I needed to work out what house-keeping meant to me, in my heart and in my head. My questions stared back at me. Was investing in home life a worthwhile thing to do? Or was it the relentless round of chores that I secretly feared it was? Was there an art to running a home, over and above folding towels into three and keeping energy use low? Was it even possible to find satisfaction in it? Would I, in years to come, be grateful for my daily rituals, my private culture of home? Or would I end my days regretting not spending more time in offices?

Gazing across the rooftops, the house lights blinking off, I wondered if my fears might be unfounded. Wasn't there a more inspiring story to tell than the one that swirled all around me? Surely it was possible to run a family home without it leading to stress and strain? To have a family and stay true to my worldly ambitions? Staring up at the stars, it didn't seem too much to ask.

Two years later, I took the leap and Paul and I married. I took a London taxi to the church and we held the reception in our flat. This time round, I was marrying for my own sake. I felt neither compelled nor compromised. I wasn't going to change my name or become a dirt-avenging housekeeper. I was confident that I could be both free and committed, and sensed that Paul felt the same. We wouldn't have to give up anything, but could just add to what we had.

The baby we conceived in Paris, three days after our wedding, set off a bomb in my unconscious. By the time the dust settled, I wasn't the same person. A layer of self-consciousness had lifted off me. My life wasn't just about me anymore. It was about us. I kept my working life alive, by training as a therapist and teaching literature part time. Even so, each morning when I woke, Alex was my first thought. I never considered my work unimportant. I was as driven by it as ever. And I always cared about the world beyond our flat. However, I felt acutely sensitive to stress and did my best to avoid it. I turned down offers to teach extra classes, and spent time making sure the girls who looked after Alex, while Paul and I were working, felt at home in our flat. Having nothing to do on the weekend became a dim memory. With a baby in tow, there was always something that needed doing. My heart and day were full and it took all I had just to stay on course.

In the months after Alex's birth, the values that Paul and I shared were tested again and again, like waves smashing against a sea wall. Values that had once been lyrical notes in our early relationship, hardened into something less forgiving. I knew, even before we started a family, that Paul didn't believe life was fair, that justice wasn't meted out according to need, and that the meek were unlikely to inherit the earth. However this belief took on a different currency once it was no longer part of our after-dinner conversations with friends, and instead threaded through our journey together with a baby.

Paul liked it when our disagreements followed a logical path, and he objected when they veered off at the tangents that I had a habit of taking.

For my part, I could be stubborn when crossed, especially around household tasks. In Paul's mind housekeeping boiled down to 'Helen's way of doing things'. I didn't care about stray socks on the floor or whether the toothpaste tube was squeezed from the top. But I did struggle to go off to sleep when there was wet laundry in the washing machine. I did pride myself on keeping a shopping list and having a stock of staples in the cupboard, especially now that there were three of us in the flat. Whereas for Paul other things were always more important than running out of dishwashing liquid.

What seemed like good domestic manners to me – picking up the bath mat after showering and wiping down the glass – flew under Paul's radar. He wasn't unsympathetic to my ways. When I explained why I'd adopted them, he respected me for it. He just didn't share them. I could have thrown my hands up in the air, and sometimes I did just this. Except that I knew Paul, who worked harder and longer at intellectual tasks than I did, wasn't lazy, or anything as simple as selfish. He cared enormously about my peace of mind. However he wasn't loyal to my way of running a home and simply didn't notice whether the bedlinen was changed.

Now that we were a family, having a household routine felt essential for my sanity. On Saturday mornings, after a walk in the park, I did the housework, putting Alex in his playpen as I vacuumed and dusted. In the afternoon, I shopped and cooked. I ordered groceries online and did my best to keep up with cooking by doubling recipes and using the freezer. I didn't mind being organised in these ways. I enjoyed having a shape to my day and keeping track of the week. I liked knowing what the days ahead held in store. But Paul, more spontaneous by nature, didn't share this feeling.

My feeling was that by giving structure to my week, I gained freedom. Having a loose routine guaranteed me pockets of time across the day. Even twenty minutes to myself was long enough to do something that made me feel real, apart from family. Ultimately I stayed loyal to my routine because, without it, housekeeping and childcare felt like a seamless, constant, pulsing thread.

I'd have liked to be more relaxed and chilled as a mother. However it was my experience that domestic tasks took place in real time, and when I didn't stay on top of them they soon got on top of me. I was without extended family in London and, despite a run of lovely students who looked after Alex when Paul and I were working, no fairy godmother appeared when I needed her most, at the end of a long day or when Alex was teething. Paul and I never came to an explicit arrangement that it was up to me to keep Alex healthy and happy, and our household running smoothly. Nonetheless, I did come to feel these things were my responsibility.

This wasn't the whole story. The flip side was that I got real pride from running our home. Creating a warm and inviting home grounded me in a way that I hadn't realised I'd been longing for. As I made a nest in our first floor flat, decorating Alex's room and brightening the kitchen, I felt inspired by all the homes that I'd visited in London, along with my childhood home. This project didn't feel at all demeaning, as I once feared it might. It felt creative, empowering even.

Every novel I'd ever taught that touched on motherhood had led me to expect that becoming a mother would lead me to feel frustrated and flatbound within months of giving birth. Within no time I'd be pining for a full-time career and plotting my return to it. But this isn't what I felt. I felt alive. I wasn't happy every minute of the day, but I did feel engaged. Compared with the stress of university teaching, which I always overprepared for, being with Alex was demanding in a way that made me feel strongly myself.

Paul, for his part, took to fathering naturally. He appreciated that I needed breaks from looking after Alex, stepping in most days to give me time to write or just walk in the park. This sympathy didn't extend to household tasks which, thanks to my competence, he continued to avoid. And so we reached an agreement. I would manage our day-to-day domestic life, and he would give me breaks from childcare and respect my way of doing things.

When Alex turned eighteen months, and I took on more teaching, Steph came to clean our flat. Every Thursday at 8am, she chained her bike to the fence and brought up her water bottle. After a quick chat, she got out the vacuum cleaner and started on the floors. Next it was the bathroom and lastly the kitchen, which she finished by wiping down the bench and sink with paper towel until they shone. Sometimes I was out teaching or counselling when Steph came, leaving Paul to cover for me. On returning home, I found the flat shining and the wooden artist's figure on the mantlepiece in the living room in a new pose. Its arms were shaped in a pirouette above its head. Its head was bowed. One foot was stretched out in a kick. I never asked Steph about this wooden figure, which moved every week. I understood that it was her way of flagging the passing of time, of saying 'Look, everything is different thanks to this one small change.' And it was.

This arrangement didn't last. Eventually Steph accepted a new job and stepped away from cleaning. I didn't mind. Because by this point, I knew something important about running our home. I understood how quickly a home could go downhill when no-one cleared the blocked drain in the bathroom, or binned the slimy lettuce at the back of the fridge. Inspired by Steph, who loved her work, I tried to do with grace those tasks which I had to do anyway. I liked feeling that I was making a positive choice, rather than having chores foisted on me. I didn't always achieve this, but I did aim for it.

4. belonging

Part of my training as a psychotherapist involved spending a day a week as an observer on an acute psychiatric ward. From our first meeting, the psychiatric patients I met on the ward seemed canny. Within days of their admission, they'd picked up from other patients the ins and outs of their care. They knew who the hard and soft nurses were, and the conditions surrounding weekend leave. Just as they knew how to turn a casual chat with a new face into a kind of quiz.

Dan, a student drop-out, introduced me to life on the ward. A forced admission after a schizophrenic episode, he was curious about me from the start. But then, with his hand on the doorknob after a twenty-minute chat, he turned on me.

'Don't you think?' he asked, eyes flashing, 'that your questions are really a way of sorting out your own problems?'

'I get that you might think that', I said. 'But I really am interested in your story.'

'Is that why you want to know about my Dad, a scum-bag who left my Mum when I was five?'

Another patient I spoke to, a gay woman in and out of mania, was just as challenging. For all her risky drug-taking – 'swashbuckling' she called it – she'd at least gone to the edge and back. And this, she announced, rightly, was further than I'd gone myself.

The Professor who arranged my psychiatric placement urged me to stay on the ward for as long as possible. 'You'll only get a feel for the place over a longer period', he said. 'If you're really going to help people, as a therapist, you need a general picture of psychiatry first.' This was the only briefing I would get. I was to observe psychiatric treatment firsthand, attend ward rounds and speak to patients when appropriate about their experience of mental illness.

Before arriving on the ward, I'd imagined a cuckoo's nest of patients strapped to metal beds, or shuffling down corridors with glazed eyes. But the mental illness that I witnessed was nothing like this. The day would start with Morning Meeting, with staff rushing down the corridor, coffee in one hand and treatment folders in the other. Twelve or so patients sauntered in after them, often in slippers and dressing gowns, to take one of the low vinyl armchairs circling the Common Room. Every Thursday this meeting held surprises. Unlike in most social situations, where what the other person will say next can be second guessed, there was no knowing what these patients might say as they flung their words into the air like tiny missiles. The doctors and nurses in the room made every effort to be pleasant. But the assembled patients would have none of it. A change in medication was making one patient's hair fall out. Room inspections, conducted at all hours, were an invasion of privacy. And there was a chorus of protest after public holidays when substandard food had been dished up.

It was striking how few of the patients seemed to mind being on the ward. Some even admitted themselves, late at night, in order to escape their bleak and lonely council flat. Lousy ward food and spot searches were worth it if, come nightfall, they felt safe, held and warm. The week after Christmas, two male patients admitted, with surprise, that they'd enjoyed the celebrations on the ward so much that there was nowhere else they'd wanted to be.

Some days, the atmosphere on the ward felt closer to that of a boarding school than a mental hospital. Once the ward rounds were out of the way, patients huddled together to chat, haggling for cigarettes and drinking tea from stained mugs. Or they'd gather around the television to catch Oprah Winfrey. Other patients, tipping into mania, danced and sang with headphones on in the corridor. A week later, the same patients would be down, as low as they'd been high, scuffing the corridor in hospital-issued foam slippers and creased pyjamas.

The more I listened to these patients' struggles, the more I understood why they might resent the staff and me. Unlike these patients, we had an advantage – and it wasn't just mental health. Before arriving on the ward, we'd made our own breakfast and chosen what to wear. We had a home to return to at the end of the day, somewhere to kick off our shoes, cook a meal and enjoy a sense of belonging that is hard to describe, yet easy to take for granted. Listening to these patients talk, I sensed how much not feeling at home, prior to their admission, had affected them. Was it possible that, before they could feel comfortable in themselves, before they could play an active role in their treatment and plan for the future, they needed a solid sense of home?

As a trainee therapist, I wasn't equipped to answer these questions. Still, they bothered me. Because, really, what was the point of offering therapy to a man who had no hot water in the flat that he was returning to? What could I possibly offer to patients who considered strong drugs, mouldy bathrooms and sedated sleep normal? The existential dilemma facing these patients seemed simple, to me at least. In order to be an individual first and patient second they needed their own sense of place. They needed a home and a circle of people who cared about them. They needed to put a key in their front door, hear it click shut behind them and feel okay about that click. And after each ward round, when the psychiatrist extended a patient's stay another week, there was a slackening of this hope.

By the time Dan and I started our weekly chats, his mental condition had been stable for two months. He seemed friendly and easy to engage. Even so, I got the sense, beneath whatever we were talking about, that his youthful ambitions were rapidly hardening into cynicism. After two months of these weekly chats, I found myself wondering why Dan was on the ward at all. I questioned his care. He had insight into his condition, which was likely triggered by a violent father, and was complying with his treatment. There seemed every reason to expect an early discharge into the hands of a community health team.

The following week, during Morning Meeting, a patient mentioned an incident between Dan and his psychiatrist, during which a three-minute argument escalated into a few seconds of aggression, leading to his being exiled to the locked ward upstairs. I sat up in my chair. I hadn't seen this coming. I'd been so busy identifying with Dan that I'd only seen his condition from his point of view. I'd assumed that he was a bit like me, which made it hard to imagine him assaulting anyone. Dan's breakdown showed the limits of my insight, which was reinforced when the psychiatrist suggested that I visit Dan upstairs – and I declined.

The Professor who arranged my placement on the ward had wanted me to experience something just like this. He'd wanted me to see how mental illness can flip a patient into becoming a danger to himself and others, no matter how together they were most of the time. This incident with Dan changed everything for me. When I looked around the ward, I saw the price that patients had paid for the plastic tag on their wrist that carried the unspoken message they were past looking after themselves, and were capable of harm. The shame and other messy feelings this triggered were as unsettling as the side-effects from the pills the nurses handed them twice a day in tiny plastic cups.

Until this point, I had treated housekeeping as essential. But still it was a chore. My experience on the ward demonstrated to me, in a lasting way, how fortunate I was to be able to cook my own meals, do my own washing and create my own sense of home.

☙

After a bad bout of flu, with assignments piling up, I found myself missing Steph's weekly visit to clean our flat. Lying in bed, I came to what seemed like the sensible conclusion that the only way I could even think about having a second child, and push on with my therapy training, was to get another cleaner. In the clear light of recovery, it seemed gloriously obvious. A friend recommended an agency and I picked up the phone and called.

Sadie, the woman the agency sent to our flat, made soup for Paul and me as we lay in bed, coughing and spluttering. Once back on my feet, she started instructing me on the ins and outs of cleaning. 'There is', she said, 'nothing a mop can do that a vacuum cleaner can't do better.' By her fourth visit, Sadie had succeeded in making me feel domestically inadequate. I came to dread the sound of her key in the front door and, as she moved through the flat, I found concentrating at my desk that much harder. Into my study she'd come, with Alex riding the barrel vacuum cleaner like a pony, as she chattered to me about her busy life. The phone in her pocket buzzed with grateful clients and her weekends revolved around multiple foster children. Three months later, on New Year's Eve, I vowed to go back to cleaning our flat myself.

My relief was immediate and lasting. I still complained about housework, but having it back to myself was a dream. Besides, the minute I started cleaning I stopped hating it. The physicality of it took me into a zone of awareness that was different from the working, mothering and social sides of myself. It was as if, as I vacuumed, a layer of self-consciousness dropped away and I tapped into a deeper source of energy. I didn't change into slippers or suck musk sweets, as my mother's cleaning woman once had. But I did feel my wits sharpen about me as I cleaned. Perhaps because I often sat at a desk, the act of cleaning had the effect of freeing up my mind. I might stop mid-vacuum to jot down the name of someone I'd been meaning to call, a friend I'd been too shy to invite for dinner, or an idea that suddenly felt pressing. Then I'd use the halo-effect, following a spate of cleaning, to act on my jotted-down list, perhaps picking up the phone and making the call that I'd been unable to make. Just an hour of cleaning left me with a sense of peace and acceptance, knowing that I'd done enough for our flat to tick over for another week. Or I might go on to change the look of a room by moving furniture about, weeding the herbs growing on the balcony, or putting oranges in a bowl in the kitchen. Anything that said, 'job well done'.

During my time in higher education, I taught various courses on the subject of gender. So I was well aware that, until the late 20th century, society valued women for their domestic competence – for the flakiness of their pie crust, the brightness of their laundry and their flower beds in spring. Thankfully, my generation was no longer judged on how well we baked, mended a fuse or gardened. Visitors to my flat didn't shame me into getting out the vacuum cleaner before they arrived. They didn't give my floors a second thought. But there was someone who did mind about the state of my flat. Over the years, my mother's critical voice seeped into and blended with my own inner voice. So that when I swept up grated cheese from the kitchen floor, wiped toothpaste from a tap, or noticed niggly things like stray peas under the kitchen table or smears on the bathroom mirror, I heard her voice in my head.

It was during my spell on the acute ward that I came to accept this about myself. I could only keep my home afloat when I looked after myself properly. If I felt resentful or frustrated as I cleaned out the fridge or hung up washing, it was because, in part, I wasn't meeting my own needs. Working in mental health was a springboard for a journey within. Rather than focusing on deadlines and must do's, I put aside time for activities that I found satisfying, for things that I'd done more of before Alex arrived and there were fewer demands on me. I left out coloured pencils on my desk ready for my next drawing. I spent time that I could have spent working pottering around our flat. And I escaped for walks in the park without Alex whenever I could.

The things I did around the flat to create a warm atmosphere started to mean more. I was making a home for my family. I wanted Alex, and Paul too, to enjoy a sense of warmth and comfort. But I was also creating a home for myself, a place where I could feel looked after and cared for. A place that inspired and held me. And this felt as real to me as the velveteen rabbit in the storybook that I kept on a shelf to read to Alex when he was a bit older. Spending time on an acute ward showed me that there were times in everyone's life when a warm and attractive home was closer to a longing than a reality. Creating a home in which we felt loved and held was an act of nurture, an ordinary magic that we weren't always up to. And it was often when we were unable to bring this about that we longed for it most.

Two years after entering the acute ward, I sat in my last Morning Meeting, five months pregnant with my second baby. I left with genuine admiration for psychiatry and for those who practice it, an awareness of the depths to which mental illness can sink vulnerable people, and a hope that I'd be able to integrate what I learned into future work.

5. self-reliance

Emma spent most of her first Christmas Eve coughing. When, at first light, her cough took on a nasty rattle, Paul and I whisked her to hospital to have her chest checked. It was snowing outside and I didn't feel at my best either. Oblivious to everything, except that it was a white Christmas, Alex was his usual bouncy self. Paul, for his part, told me that the crisis would soon pass and that there were lots of Christmases to come.

In need of sympathy, I phoned my mother, twelve hours behind in Australia, to share my woes with her. When I finished speaking, there was a pause. 'You know', she said, 'you're so lucky to have a second child. And a girl at that. I'm sure Emma will be just fine. And, until then, you'll just have to grin and bear it.' We chatted about other things, wished each other a happy Christmas, and I hung up with her phrase, 'you'll just have to grin and bear it', ringing in my ears.

Mum hadn't offered to drop everything to umbrella into our upstairs flat, like Mary Poppins, to nurse her eleventh grandchild. Instead she'd told me that there are some things, like a newborn with bronchitis, that have to be endured. Her tone was matter of fact. I would have to put up with reality as it was. With that single phrase about soldiering on, Mum handed over her baton to me. Rather than offering the comfort I longed for and that she'd given me as a child, she told me to find strength within. Just as she must have done, I realised, as I waited for the kettle to boil in my galley kitchen, when she herself became a mother.

For weeks, in the lead up to Christmas, I'd fantasised about waking up surrounded by little ones and unwrapping presents, about listening to carols while chopping vegetables. I hadn't pictured putting saline drops into Emma's tiny nostrils and steaming my own, stooped under a towel in the bathroom.

I had what I wanted, two wonderful children and a loving husband. This made it harder to distract myself with fantasies of good things to come. It was a different kind of challenge I faced: to be creative with what I had, finding satisfaction in that. Mum had hinted that she had nothing more to give me that I couldn't give myself. Whatever I might want – my wildest dreams and grandest ambitions – would now have to take its place alongside what I could manage emotionally, from moment to moment and from day to day. All of this was wrapped up in the lesson of coping with my sick newborn at Christmas.

I picked up my phone and cancelled lunch with friends. Then I turned up the gas fire and threw a rug on the floor for an inside picnic. Alex was none the wiser and Paul was happy to play along. There was no turkey, no cranberry sauce and no crackers. And yet after a few games and messing around, we had as much fun as on any other Christmas. Pulling the curtains against the early dark, we watched *Chitty Chitty Bang Bang* on the couch. It wasn't my fantasy Christmas. It was something else. And it felt all the better for being real.

Being the mother of small children forced me into a self-reliance I hadn't known I was capable of. My mother's advice, that short sharp shock that she was so good at, woke me from a slumber I hadn't known I was in. Rather than waiting for someone else to create Christmas, it was time to create it myself. The push for better things had been inside me all along. Family life was bringing it into the light.

I'd always known that if I had a family I would embrace a nurturing role. For years, this knowledge had made me wary of motherhood. Why on earth, asked the voice in my head, would I want to be needed to the point of indispensability to my family? Because, my answer rang out, sitting by the fire that Christmas night, my desire for a deep connection to family, and the creativity it sparked, felt deeply satisfying.

CB

The following Christmas, during a trip to Adelaide to introduce Emma to my family, the four of us stayed with friends in the country. Keen for an early start, our host Sally left out breakfast things for us in the kitchen. After eating and washing up, we wandered outside to glimpse Sally pushing a wheelbarrow around the corner of the house. Wearing shorts, work boots and an old straw hat, she looked, to my city-dweller eye, like a frontier woman from a novel I might be teaching, bronzed and determined to beat the odds. Her silhouette, with loaded wheelbarrow and morning sun behind, captured everything I felt I was missing out on in a London flat. A large vegetable garden with summer sweetcorn and basil. A proper compost heap. Hens scratching in the yard. A way of life that, until I glimpsed Sally in her cut-off shorts and work boots, I hadn't known I longed for. Shoveling manure on to garden beds is a labouring job. Yet there was no sense that Sally was made menial by it. There was a quiet dignity, a sense of calm and order, of things being as they should be, despite a world in flux just beyond the farm gate. I knew this kind of serenity was fleeting, but I couldn't help but want it for myself.

On returning to London, all I could think about was those chickens scratching in the yard. I dreamed about planting from seeds and making bread from a sack of flour. 'The domestic arts', my friends asked, a query lifting their voices, 'what exactly do you mean?' I understood their confusion. Cooking, sewing, renovating, craft and gardening, these had been commercialised, sentimentalised, or buried alive under the gremlin we called housework. Determined not to follow in our mothers' footsteps, the multitude of tasks that sustain a home worth loving had been reduced to the weekly chores of keeping it clean and tidy. The art of running a home had been siphoned off into a lifestyle option, squeezed into hours that we didn't have, using energy that we resented not spending on more rewarding activities.

Like the rest of my friends in London, I was drawn to ideas, imagination and higher things, and not to meal plans and household budgets. I didn't exactly despise practicality. I simply assumed that my future lay in the world beyond my home. However, now that I was running my own family home, my youthful search for higher things no longer felt like the whole story. Surely, I asked myself, as I put our flat to rights, if I can satisfy the necessities of life in good spirit, the meaning of life will take care of itself? The problem was that, depending on my mood, I felt split between the down-to-earth and questing sides of myself. I wanted a buoyant home life, of course I did, but I also wanted to be free to pursue my ambitions in the world. Too often, this felt impossible to do.

Circling our flat at dusk, I pulled blinds, turned down beds and started on dinner. Ushering in the evening ahead, I was making our flat into a home. As I greeted Paul when he came through the front door, I kept an eye on the hob while picking out shoes from the mound of kids' clothes by the bathroom door. Going about these tasks, a thorny question crossed my mind. Was there dignity in these homely acts? Or was it closer to resignation? Could I feel both?

Housekeeping wasn't a shared way of life that I chatted about with friends when we met up. I often asked them how their work was going. And I always asked after the people they loved and cared about most. But I never asked, even close friends, how they felt about running their home, or the atmosphere they were seeking to create there. Cooking was an easy enough topic of conversation. But creating a home seemed so personal, so sensitive and huge a topic that I felt reluctant to probe. It would be rude to ask someone about their style in interiors, how they felt about growing things, and that perennial conversation stopper, housework. And yet, of course, the more my thoughts turned to the home, the more it struck me that everyone I was speaking to was, like me, spending up to a quarter of their waking hours doing the same.

Rising above my resistance to household tasks that didn't delight, and doing them well, had become a source of self-esteem for me. Yet many of my closest friends had either scaled back their domestic life or successfully outsourced it. And so while the work I did at home felt essential to me, this wasn't reflected among the people around me. This felt disorienting and lonely. It made me wonder if my life, in so far as it was shaped by the home, was a lesser thing.

This prompted big questions. If I wasn't housekeeping to meet social expectations, which had loosened a lot since I was a girl, what was I housekeeping for? Why didn't I just apply for more teaching to cover the cost of a cleaner? More to the point, *who* was I housekeeping for? Was it to stay one step ahead of my inner critic who, never quite satisfied with my efforts, contaminated my free time with a stream of musts and shoulds? Or was it to keep aloft a family and home that the heavens had seen fit to bless me with?

Each time I puffed up doonas, gathered dirty clothes and put our flat to rights, it was because I felt that an attractive home was worth keeping up. Clearing away clutter and giving clothes to charity was something that I did for my own peace of mind. Like so many other things relating to the home, my satisfaction was my guide. This was a giant shift. Previously, I'd relied on external validation for my efforts. The annual review of my work in the university department I taught in, a footnote to a journal article of mine, the number of stars next to an online book review. In contrast to these achievements, I received little feedback at home. Friends might say something nice about our flat when they came for dinner, but that was about it.

Family life had outed me. Having kept quiet about my love of home throughout my 20s, I now embraced it. I didn't like everything about it, but I felt it was worth the effort. I wanted our home life to have a buoyancy that supported us even when we were off doing other things. I wanted our own rituals of home, our own ways of celebrating our place in the world. I wanted the hours that we spent at home to mean something, even if I had to invent some of this meaning myself.

As I looked around our London flat, it seemed cramped to me. There wasn't enough room to expand or experiment. One day, folding down the table in our galley kitchen, I was chatting to Alex about his upcoming third birthday and he asked what kind of cake I was planning to make. 'But', I blurted out, 'I don't have time to make a cake!' In an instant, Alex's eyes pooled with tears and he rushed from the room. I followed, but he'd have none of my apologies. 'You're always busy', he said, accusingly. 'I'm sorry', I said. 'Of course I have time to make you a cake. Especially if we can make it together.' 'Really?' he said, looking up and wiping his nose on his sleeve.

How had this happened? And how might I create a home in which making a birthday cake didn't feel like one more thing to be ticked off before I could feel halfway good about myself? I wanted baking to be the crazy joy it had been growing up, when my younger sister and I made wacky birthday cakes together. A gingerbread house with Smarties dripping off the roof, a wonky igloo, a forest scene. The more elaborate and sweet-laden the better. It was only since leaving Adelaide that I'd lost touch with this zany side of myself, bent as I was on forging a path to a proper career.

And so it was that I began plotting another kind of life, with space for line-dried sheets and a linen cupboard to store them in. A life with more space and time in it. While it would be easy to put down my dilemma to living in a tight London flat with two small children, a writer husband and not enough cake tins, the crux of my dilemma was more profound. Perhaps I'd felt the joy of baking, as a girl, because when I was young the necessities of life had been taken care of by my mother? Perhaps I was struggling to look after myself and my family because, in fantasy, some-one else, off in the wings, did it for me. In my fantasies of home, there was always a loving other in the background who did the domestic things that I was reluctant to do myself – bake the cake, unpack the groceries and generally carry the domestic load. But now that I was the mother of small children myself, I had less time for fantasies. Besides, I'd had a cleaner in the past, and so knew that earning more to pay someone to share my domestic load wasn't my answer. In my brave new world of motherhood, it was simpler to captain my own ship.

Ever since I brought Alex home from hospital, one chilly afternoon, looking after my family had been a huge thing for me. I think this was because it meant assuming enough maturity to create a rich home life – nourishing meals, warm beds and stacks of clean underwear – without counting its cost to the rest of my life. For years I'd been on the receiving end of this kind of practical loving from scores people, starting with my mother in childhood. However, being on the cake-making end still felt fairly new. I'd always known that I'd find being a mother demanding. But until this exchange with Alex in the kitchen I'd somehow overlooked how demanding it was to run a family home. If I was going to be the mother I wanted to be, and to run the kind of home that I wanted to run, something would have to give.

A week before my next birthday I had an appointment with a specialist for a recurring sinus infection. As the doctor carried out various tests, I mentioned my upcoming birthday, adding that I didn't know what to make of getting older. The doctor looked up, smiled and took off his glasses. 'You know', he said, 'I hardly notice when my birthday comes around. In my experience, if you like what you do and are happy with the overall direction of your life, your birthday just slips by.' I smiled back, thinking to myself how glad I was that he'd studied medicine and not psychology.

On the morning of my birthday, the wind whistling through the trees, the idea of leaving London was born. We were on holiday in Scotland, visiting Paul's family. Alex and Emma woke us early, rumpling and bouncing on the bed. 'What if we woke up to the sound of trees outside the window every day?' I asked Paul, after the kids disappeared to play. 'Absolutely', said Paul, who'd forgotten how lovely country life could be. In the end, nothing dramatic led to our decision to move to Australia. We'd been inching towards it since starting a family. It was more a dawning awareness that the possibilities available to us as a family in North London were limited – even finding Alex a school was a small nightmare – and that a more generous life beckoned to us from leafy Melbourne.

CႣ

My friend Anita and I had arranged to meet in a café in the heart of the city, halfway between our respective flats, to discuss our writing projects. Every fortnight, for the last three years, it had been the same. This time, hurrying from the tube station, I considered how I would break my news to Anita. I would be diplomatic. I wouldn't just blurt out our decision to leave. But within minutes of ordering tea and sitting down, I announced our departure in a sentence. Anita looked up and put down her cup. Her face looked cross. This wasn't, she pointed out, a perhaps that I was presenting her with. It was a decision that she'd been left out of. Of course, she said quickly, she wanted the best for me. But she wanted the best for herself, too. 'How can we go on discussing each other's work, if you're in another country?' 'We can email', I said, trying to sound upbeat. 'And we can plan to visit every other year.' Anita glanced across the table, a quizzical look on her face. In that moment, we both knew, without the need for words, that our friendship would never be the same. I already had two children to Anita's one, which had stretched and deepened our working relationship. But moving to another country was different. It was a statement of intent, proof that I was willing to live without her altogether.

Our decision to leave London seemed sudden to others, too. It wasn't just Anita. Paul's parents and our circle of friends made it clear that our leave-taking was abrupt. Yet in my heart I knew that it was no whim. For years, I'd wanted to live somewhere where the sun shone, the beaches were long, Paul and I might find work, and our kids could roam freely. I also felt ready to take on a house and garden, to express a domestic side that had lain dormant for so long. I felt as grown up as I'd ever be, and wanted my home life to reflect this. It was time to grow the flowers that I picked for the windowsill.

6. apron

The first time I walked into our house in Melbourne, I felt elated. After a year-long search it was, despite fronting on to a busy road, the kind of house I'd hoped we might find, with a big kitchen, sunny verandah, compost heap and washing line. A sandstone Victorian with a decent back garden, it was in every way a proper house. The sitting room overlooked the road, and the windows of the kitchen and living room opened out to a balcony. After sanding the timber floors to blond, we put down our London rugs and hung up cream curtains. The house felt solid and roomy, yet cosy too. We gave Alex the master bedroom, in the hope that it would be big enough for Emma and him to play in and to house their toys. The kids loved the house, playing happily for hours at a time, which freed me up to complete the renovations after we moved in.

The young woman who left Australia for London in her early 20s would have been surprised to know that, on returning, her keenest moments of satisfaction, her greatest release from daily cares, would be found at home. I now got more satisfaction from a weekend burst of gardening, or sewing at the kitchen table, than from visiting dance clubs or art galleries. After years of living in small flats, just the fact of lying in bed between sun-dried sheets felt blessed.

Moving back to Australia for a better quality of life gave me permission to care about what I'd always cared about. Though I was teaching literature part-time, my identity felt more closely tied to who I was and what I did around the house than to what I got up to at my desk. Now that Alex was old enough to awaken my memories of being his age, as if from nowhere, a less defended side of myself emerged. I felt drawn to the same domestic arts – cooking, sewing, renovating and gardening – that, as a girl, I'd thought best to avoid. Nurturing my home and family wasn't the bind that I imagined it would be when I was growing up. It gave a lot back. Even the worm farm in the garage was a welcome challenge. Except for one thing. Which is that while I had more space than I ever had in London, I didn't have more time. I had the same number of hours in the day, but now with growing kids and a house to look after.

In the opening pages of Homer's famous story, Odysseus sets out on his epic journey, leaving his wife at home in Ithaca. Many romantic encounters and brushes with death later, the hero returns home to find that his wife has spent the time keeping suitors at bay and weaving at her loom. First as a student then as a lecturer, whenever this story was discussed in university seminars I identified with Ulysses. Never with Penelope, his stay-at-home wife. I would never slay a double-headed monster, but it seemed natural to assume that a life of adventure lay ahead. It never crossed my mind that I might one day be left holding the fort while my husband travelled the world for work, slaying his own metaphysical dragons. It never dawned on me that family life might take me on a journey to the world of the familiar, the known, and that I might find there unexplored treasures. And that, on this journey, my sympathies would shift from the questing Odysseus to the resourceful Penelope.

I had changed. Overcoming my reluctance for household tasks that didn't delight, yet I felt were worth doing, gave me as strong a sense of credit as meeting work deadlines. Growing vegetables from seed and simmering chicken stock on the hob, came to feel like achievements. My tussles with home work had led me to value it more, now that I knew how challenging it is to run a family home. Keeping several balls in the air – housekeeping, family and work – felt like an accomplishment. And no less, an act of love.

Even with this reckoning, it wasn't plain sailing. I still wrestled with household tasks. Putting away laundry and getting the vacuum cleaner fixed, these still took up more time in my mind than the time it took to actually do them. Like everyone I knew, I had a prejudice against repeated domestic tasks. Sweeping the kitchen floor felt like a chore, while doing yoga stretches felt like a reward for early rising. I was yet to realise that when I whined about a particular task, my complaint was mostly made up of the feelings I projected on to it, rather than the task itself. Vacuuming the kitchen floor took me a few minutes at most. Putting off vacuuming the floor, cursing the crumbs under the chairs and wishing the floor would magically clean itself, this consumed more time and energy than getting out the vacuum and switching it on.

Initially I was reluctant to wear an apron when I cooked and cleaned. I wanted to protect my clothes from oil spills, but I worried what others might think of me wearing one. I worried about what *I* thought about wearing one. And yet as soon as my apron was tied, I stopped dithering and got on with whatever I was doing. Wearing an apron showed me that, in the right frame of mind, housekeeping was no more drudge-inducing than an hour at the gym. In a good mood, cleaning the house generated as many endorphins as hiking up a hill.

With this shift in awareness, I started valuing my efforts around the house a lot more. Rather than treating tasks as thankless chores, I set a timer and made them into a game. Or I used the time I spent housekeeping to keep track of the thoughts that ran through my mind – listening to them one by one, rather than being pulled every which way by them, a human tumbleweed. So that, on a good day, housekeeping became an active form of meditation. I took my apron off feeling less stressed than when I put it on. I worked physically harder than I ever had in London. Yet I felt more earthed. Planting broad beans before a rain cloud broke, or unblocking an outside drain, grotty job that it was, made me feel, in some elemental way, part of the order of things.

I never felt that the domestic side of myself was more important than what I got up to at my desk or in the classroom. But then nor did I feel that my intellectual efforts were more important than my home work. Both were essential to me. Besides, they were such different things, which may be why I felt no call to devote myself to one over the other. Relinquishing my hopes for a work-life balance came at a price, however. It meant inhabiting the split between home and work, love and ambition, consciously, with my eyes open.

In the months that followed, I railed less at Paul and our kids to do more around the house. Instead I did more yoga. I learned to live with the tension that I'd discovered at the heart of home life. Until, without noticing, I stopped wishing it away. It was just the way my life was. I made peace with how things were and embraced the not-quite-rightness of my life. Instead of trying to solve my domestic riddle, home became the place where the wild things were. And while I still didn't define myself by what I did at home, I sometimes wondered how much it was shaping me, altering me. Could I be curious about this shift? Could it take me to new places without ever leaving home?

When Paul published a book about the history of civilization, after many painstaking drafts, I went to a talk that he gave about it. As the lights in the auditorium dimmed, he quoted one of the characters from Tolstoy's *War and Peace* who believed that the purpose of civilization was to make the necessities of life into sources of satisfaction. Yes, I thought, puffing after running from the car, that would be nice. What struck me, that hot afternoon, was that I wanted this idea to be true. I wanted to find satisfaction in the necessities that shaped my days.

In many ways, I did find it. Absorbed in household tasks, mixed feelings didn't bother me. Seeing the light shine off dusted furniture felt like its own reward. Even changing the bloated vacuum cleaner bag felt pleasing, knowing that it was plump with dust from our floors. Looking after our house led me to possess it more intimately than renovating it had. And I loved going out into the garden, on finishing the housework for the week, and sitting down with a cup of tea. Stretching out on the grass, I felt at peace. I was part of the world around me: of night and day; clean and dirty; summer and winter; young and old. And I really liked that feeling.

Up on the stage, Paul was projecting on to a screen an oil painting by Australian impressionist Fred McCubbin. In this painting, Paul told the audience, the artist has captured a woman daydreaming as she shells a bowl of peas. At that moment, an older woman behind me shot up her hand. 'What if that woman by the window doesn't like shelling peas? What if she'd rather be outside taking a walk before dinner?' Paul paused, his hand fell to his side, and he laughed. 'Sure', he said, 'you may be right.' Then he moved on to his next slide. I felt torn. I wanted to agree with Paul that shelling peas offered a pleasant lull in the late afternoon, but I couldn't help siding with the woman behind me who thought that a walk at dusk might be preferable.

By this point, my family and I had lived in another big city for eight years. Our kids were growing like kelp, challenging Paul and me at every turn. What I kept hitting against, like an automatic door that wouldn't open, was what I came to think of as the paradox of nurture. My desire to nurture family, to be warm, generous and practically loving, wasn't reciprocated by the family to whom I was devoted. Satisfying the demands of family and home fell largely to me. And, as rewarding as I found running a home to be, at times this arrangement made me feel that my wings had been clipped at the same time that my heart had been prised open.

At the end of the talk, as Paul fielded questions from the audience, I considered the choices before me. I could resist my nurturing side and demand a fairer share from my family. This seemed like the sensible choice. I could insist on a better arrangement with my undomestic husband who might offer to pay half for a cleaner. Another sensible choice. Or I could do something more risky, and stay on the road I was already on. I could direct some of my ambitions onto my home and seek meaning there. I could embrace my kids' need for me, for food on the table and clean sheets in the cupboard, and so take my place on the wheel of life, safe in the knowledge that it wouldn't last forever.

This last option went against all the advice I'd received. Yet sitting in the auditorium, as the lights came up, it felt right to me. I didn't feel proud of taking this path. I knew, even then, that I'd always feel complicated about choosing it. But nor did I feel ashamed that, when it came to a conflict this intimate, this essential, my heart defeated my head. I would embrace the paradox of nurture, the nonreciprocal nature of family love, at the heart of home life. I would stop drinking my own poison and cease to resent Paul's and my kids' avoidance of the domestic. And in leaning into this realm, I would discover what, if anything, was to be found there.

7. house exchange

My friendship with Anita did change when I moved to Melbourne, a city I knew that she was unlikely, for financial reasons, ever to visit. But not all the changes were bad. Keeping in frequent email contact gave our friendship a new intensity. A few months after we arrived in Melbourne, while Paul and I were busy house-hunting, Anita had her second book published. Then she sent news that she was toying with having a second child. Until one afternoon, out of the blue, I received an email from her saying that she'd been to the doctor after finding a lump in her breast and that the tests had come back positive. I stared at the screen, willing that word positive into its opposite.

In the months that followed, I supported Anita from afar, privately railing against an ailing health system that seemed to be willfully dropping my friend through its cracks. During multiple treatments, Anita remained strong. After painstakingly researching her condition, she set about beating her lengthening odds. But as the months became a year, the tone of her emails changed. She sounded woolly, out of reach. It took a few weeks of heartbreak, of staring blankly at her emails as first her grammar then her spelling went, to realise that she had let me go. Now that it was a matter of life and death, our long-distance friendship couldn't support her. She drew into her family and started chanting at her local church. She was making the most of each day and I was too far away to be of help. Emails were pointless, I needed to visit.

Searching for places to stay near London, I chanced on a house-exchange website and was quickly drawn in. It seemed like the best of both worlds, exotic yet also pragmatic. I found flicking through photos of other people's homes seductive. I could wake up in the middle of Chelsea in a cobblestone mews, peeking out over chimney pots. I could lie on the grass of a blue-stone cottage on the outskirts of Edinburgh, with the moors a short drive away. Or we could stay in a flat overlooking Brighton Pier, a stone's throw from Anita's house.

Right from the start, I liked that I was joining a club in which trust triumphed over paranoia. I got that it involved exchanging homes, and not houses or flats. But Paul took the opposite view. For him, a house exchange lay somewhere between leaving our front door ajar and wearing second-hand shoes. It took a good few weeks of emailing him house listings when he was at work to persuade him that an exchange might work for us.

If three years hadn't gone by since I'd last seen English friends and Paul's family, I might have given up the idea of an exchange at this point. But the prospect of spending six weeks seeing Anita, along with old friends and family, without breaking the bank, seemed worth any effort. Even so, I knew that exchanging homes would involve more than buying a new chopping board, topping up on tea towels and sticking a note to the fridge. When I mentioned an exchange to friends, more than one promptly replied, 'What a great idea.' As if just hearing about our exchange might inspire them to rush home and set up their own. But I knew that few, if any, would. Because by this stage in my research I knew that fantasising about an exchange was easy but signing off on one was hard.

Uploading attractive photos, and writing an inviting house listing, was more challenging than I thought it would be. It meant looking at our home in a newly critical light. It meant looking into the cutlery drawer and spying crumbs under the spoons, just as a visitor might. Only, unlike a visitor, it meant upending the drawer and wiping it out. It meant mend-ing the broken blind in the kitchen, screwing the bathroom door back on its hinges, and scrubbing off the kids' finger marks running hip height the length of the hall.

Combing through and freshening up our house reminded me of putting our London flat on the market. Except the real estate agent who sold our flat there never had to sleep in our bed, or peer into the fridge. He didn't have to hunt through the linen cupboard in the middle of the night, as a home exchanger might, looking for clean sheets for a sick child. Coming back inside, after pulling the garden into shape, I looked around our house. Would another family feel at home there? Would they feel welcome? Could they relax and have fun? Was the love I felt for our home plain enough that visitors would look after it, respect it?

There were plenty of how-to guides to home exchange on the web, and I read them avidly. It doesn't matter, they said, if your home is more modest than your exchanger's, as long as it's as clean and well presented as it appears in your photos. It doesn't matter if you have one bathroom and they have two, as long as they know in advance. It doesn't matter if they're semi-retired and you have a young family, as long as they're comfortable with kids playing in their living room. But it really does matter, every guide urged, if you suddenly change your dates, or tease your exchangers with flattering photos that lead their hearts to sink when they open your front door, weary from travel.

Late at night, when I should have been asleep, I flipped through hundreds of listings. Like an online dater, I was looking for something I couldn't put into words. A top-floor flat in Edinburgh made me wonder why we'd ever moved to Melbourne, while a dour '60s red-brick semi in Bristol instantly confirmed why we had. I felt prompted to everything from scorn for indoor jacuzzis, to a longing I didn't know I had for cottage gardens in small villages.

Members on the site described themselves in breezy tones, laying out their careers, families and homes from end to end for all to see. 'Mother of three, childcare assistant and yoga instructor.' 'Semi-retired teacher with builder partner and a shared love of travel.' Nothing in their listings led me to imagine them lying in bed in the small hours, wondering how their life might turn out. Unlike me, they didn't scramble to pay monthly bills or despair of their kids ever growing up. They were sensible couples who earmarked money for their kids' higher education and organised holidays a year ahead. They were double incomers who had the roof repaired the week it sprang a leak, and blocked out dates for filing taxes as a matter of course. But then, one evening, I idly clicked on my own listing and realised that I sounded just as credible as every other home exchanger. We were all marketing ourselves, as much as we were marketing our homes.

On beginning my search, I felt quietly smug that I lived in a lovely house in a leafy part of Melbourne. Three bedrooms, two bathrooms and a garden. What more could anyone want? A few days of searching made it clear just how much our home lacked: no television; no microwave; no spare bedroom; and no air conditioning. We lived on a busy road near a motorway entrance. I started to worry. What if no-one wanted a house in the Melbourne suburbs in the middle of summer without a beach in sight?

Thankfully, a few people did. Within three days, two members made contact. Feeling each other out, we sent more photos, nervous that one of us might make an offer before the other was ready to commit. Surely I wasn't the only one to think twice about the strangeness of sleeping in someone else's bedroom? The first exchanger to make an offer seemed a little too eager, a bit too pally, or just more experienced? Whatever it was, something in our communication didn't feel right and I pulled back. I soon realised that, more important than the number of bedrooms and the use of a car, was ease of communication. With that, I stopped searching for accommodation in outer London with a spare room for my in-laws, and looked for an exchanger with a similar approach to life – friendly yet tentative, house proud but not fastidious.

Sarah reached out. From our first email contact, I liked her. Sarah was that mercurial thing, someone a bit like me. Like me, she had young children and worked part-time. And like me she didn't want to obsess about leaving her house in a pristine state. We hardly knew each other, but we had these things in common, and it sealed our agreement. I checked her references and, in seconds, the internet put my mind to rest. Two days later, Sarah and I signed off on a six-week home exchange.

As the exchange shifted from idea to reality, my mood moved from excitement to apprehension. Now I really would have to do something about the mess under the kitchen sink, and a flurry of other things.

The night before our flight to London, I awoke from a bad dream. In the dream, we arrived for a home exchange in Paris to find that the family we were exchanging with were still at home in their pyjamas, with no plans to leave. This wasn't the scary bit. The corner of the apartment that had been photographed for the exchange site looked warm, intimate and attractive. A table lamp lit a reading chair in front of a wood-burning stove. A rug covered the polished concrete floor. A vase of flowers was on the table and a book lay open. Except, in the dream, this was the only appealing corner of the apartment. The rest looked like a one-star motel that would be fine for a couple of nights, but depressing for six weeks, with fluorescent strip lighting, vinyl-covered furniture and a '50s kitchen.

I'm not someone who normally stuffs things into cupboards before visitors are due, wishing away mess by scraping it into drawers, on top of cupboards, and under the bathroom basin. But the next morning in the hour before our taxi to the airport, I did just this. I was like a character in Tolstoy's *War and Peace*, forced to flee Moscow before Napoleon's invading army. Only, instead of throwing my valuables on top of a waiting cart, I stashed library books, work files, photos, sandy sandals and damp towels in my study, now the no-go room. Against one wall a temporary clothes rack, assembled before breakfast by Alex, listed to the left under the weight of the clothes that I had shifted from our wardrobe so that Sarah and her husband could hang their clothes and feel at home.

Thirty hours later, we turned the key in the lock of Sarah's house and I felt a rush of gratitude. Sarah's house in Windsor in no way resembled my bad dream. The photos on the website closely matched her actual home. It was, in every way, the kind of narrow Victorian house that we might have lived in ourselves, had we left London for a smaller city in the UK five years earlier.

On first glance, Sarah and her family seemed much like my family and me. A quick read of their bookshelf confirmed my hunch. There was, however, one big difference. Everything was out on display. Nothing – the baby car seat, the dirty washing – had been put away in a no-go room. Sarah and her family might have popped out to the shops, or gone off to work like the three bears, and could arrive back at any time. The only outward sign they'd been gone for a while was that the house was freezing.

Hunting for matches to light the gas fire, I opened the cupboard next to the fireplace. In that second, books, photos, Christmas presents, manila folders and more books toppled out. It was the same in the kitchen, although no attempt at stacking there had been made. Things swirled about in drawers. In the drawer next to the hob I found keys, birthday candles, an empty Aspirin packet, Wiggles concert tickets, school reminders, recipe cards, library fines, gum wrappers, squeezed flat ointment tubes, empty window envelopes, sunglasses and stray playing cards. The silent chaos of family life all in one drawer. And, hooray, a box of matches.

As I lit the gas fire, there was a crash from above. Bounding up the stairs, I found Alex in the dormer bedroom, stuck under a wardrobe that had fallen on him. 'I only wanted this plane', he sniffed, holding up a model of a DC10 plane as I lifted books and toys off him. We didn't even try to put everything that fell out of the wardrobe back in. Pushing everything into a corner of the room, we sat down on the bottom bunk. 'Look at those stars', said Alex, admiringly, pointing at the plastic fluorescent stars stuck to the ceiling, an arm's length from the top bunk. 'Lovely', I said, hoping they wouldn't shine too brightly at bed-time. Even on holiday, particularly on holiday, I was a mother.

By the end of our first evening, I'd dropped my 'people like us' theory. Sarah and I had young children and worked part-time. However, a few hours in her house made it clear that she didn't care about the kind of domestic things that I cared about. And why should she? She, I imagined, cared about more important things, the state of her soul and the children starving in Africa (photos of foster children were perched on bookshelves), and not about folded sheets, well-stocked cupboards and a clean fridge. I had to laugh. The trouble I'd gone to spring cleaning my kitchen and making space in the wardrobe, these reflected my standards, not Sarah's.

Just because I'd thought it was good manners to clear out our car and blitz the kitchen, why should she? Sarah had probably stored things under beds and on top of cupboards all her life, not just in readiness for our visit. She had three children under seven to my more manageable two. Perhaps, I thought, if I'd gone on to have a third child, I too would be slipping every stray item into a drawer.

After sleeping a few nights in Sarah's sagging double bed on a foam overlay that made Paul and I sweat despite the snow outside, I bought a cotton mattress protector, fully knowing it was too bulky to take home. I did however manage to resist calling in a plumber to fix the dripping taps in the bathroom. In my heart these were just details. The main thing was that Sarah and I had trusted each other enough to exchange homes. Every time we spoke on the phone about something or other – Melbourne is wintry, is there a spare heater; Windsor is freezing, can we boost the boiler – there was no impatience, just friendly instruction.

Two days after our arrival, Paul and I had a party. Before leaving Melbourne, I sent out invitations to old friends. Not for a moment did I think they'd all come. But as Sunday afternoon passed into evening, the house swelled with people. A band of excited children flew paper planes off the garden wall on to the snowy grass below. It was overwhelming to have in one room so many friends I feared we'd lost. At the end of the night, even knowing I would see Anita the next day, I worried that I might never see other friends again. I felt like barring those remaining from leaving. But I needn't have worried. As it turned out, three years is no time at all in a long friendship.

Next morning I came downstairs to white kitchen tiles streaked brown with mud. Chips were trodden into the shaggy rug in the living room and, on the deck, plastic furniture was upturned for use as a climbing frame. But there was a bigger problem that couldn't be fixed with a mop, bucket and vacuum cleaner. The back lawn, the day before blanketed with snow, had been turned to slurry under small frantic feet. Like a teenager after a party, with parents due home, I panicked. The kitchen was easy enough to clean up. But that muddy lawn defied me. Short of reseeding it in the deep of winter, I could only hope that spring would be kind.

The number one rule of house exchange is that you treat your exchangers' property as if your own. This I had done. In the middle of a party, it didn't occur to me to stop thrill-seeking kids jumping off a garden wall on to the grass below. I didn't think to stop Alex from covering up the fluorescent stars on his bedroom ceiling with duct tape after they kept him awake. Tape which, on removing it at the end of our stay, brought triangles of ceiling paint with it. And we all had a hand in scraping two parallel grooves into the sandstone hearth as we dragged out the grate to light the gas fire.

As much as I relaxed into Sarah's house, it never felt like home. I loved my home in a way that I couldn't love another's. I made allowances for its quirks that I despaired of in Sarah's, like the Laundromat four blocks away which only took one-pound coins. How Sarah expected me to wash our sheets and towels – her express request – before our early flight to Scotland, I'll never know. Equally Sarah must have cursed our decision to replace all the overhead lights in our house with floor lamps, causing them to fumble in the dark for light switches.

Anita and her family came to our party in Windsor. But they came late and Anita was one among twenty-five guests. Two days later, I knocked at her front door, after missing the right exit on the motorway. Anita opened it and we hugged. Then she stepped back to survey me. 'Isn't that the same jacket you used to wear in London?' she asked, implying that a new jacket was the least I could do after years away. I laughed but saw her point. It was a high street woollen jacket that had lost its edge. But Anita and I both knew that my jacket was beside the point. Whereas I looked pretty much the same as when I left London, Anita's body had thickened from the steroid treatment she was having. Thankfully, her hair had grown back dark and glossy after chemo. Her brown eyes sparkled and her skin, though pale, was clear. The biggest difference was on the inside. In place of her old determination, something softer, kinder perhaps, had taken its place.

The physical toll from Anita's treatment became obvious when we went out to explore the neighbourhood and she barely made it around the block. A bigger shock came at lunch time. A life-long foodie, she no longer cared what she ate. 'Would you mind rustling up something for us to eat?' she asked, waving her hand towards a small bar fridge. 'I can't taste a thing, and mealtimes come around so quickly.'

Anita's husband was looking after his wife as best he could, while working in London and picking up the slack with their son. They'd pulled together as a couple, and were doing their best to hold together a loving and workable family life. Washing up after lunch, it occurred to me that there was no-one else to look after Anita and her family. Her mother came and went, but she couldn't be there all the time. More than this, there was no-one to put things right now that so much had gone wrong. Anita may never recover and everyone in her home knew it. Her child might lose his mother, her husband might lose his wife. That this could happen out of the blue, to my closest friend, with her sharp mind, beautiful soul and gritty resolve, felt like a knife in my heart.

After lunch, Anita took me into her tiny garden. Holding my hand, her voice brightened. 'When we first moved in, this courtyard was full of junk', she said, waving an upturned hand from left to right. 'It was a battle just to get through the door. During that first year, when I was working in London and rushing back to pick up Tom from school, I couldn't face clearing it. Gardening wasn't on the top of my list. It wasn't even on my list. But since my treatment I've been coming out every day. I have coffee out here after walking Tom to school. I especially love it in spring, when everything I cut back before winter starts shooting again.' She broke off, searching my face. 'I know it's not much, barely even a garden. Nothing compared with what you must have in Melbourne.' She looked away, tears in her eyes. 'But for me it's everything.'

I drove back to Windsor without turning on the radio. Without saying anything, Anita had told me that it didn't matter how big a garden I had, if I didn't have eyes to see it. It didn't matter how much space I had to grow flowers and vegetables, if I missed the wonder and delight that she felt for her handkerchief garden. In treasuring her rosemary, and in refusing to give in to fear, Anita gave me more than she knew.

For the next five weeks we made ourselves at home in Windsor. By the last week, there wasn't a board game we hadn't played, no cupboard we hadn't peered into. We bought gum boots and got muddy in the Great Park, trudging home with head-torches in the dark. We explored London museums by day and retreated to our warm nest at night, sometimes persuading friends to join us. I forgave myself for our minor damage and the lawn survived our visit. And I spent two more days with Anita, it was all she was up to. By the time we locked up Sarah's house, I felt excited about the life we were returning to. But sad, too, for the life we were leaving behind. We'd been lucky to be able to return to it, even for a brief time.

After leaving Windsor, we spent the weekend with neighbours from London who'd moved to an Essex farmhouse when we left for Australia. Jo is an old friend, which is why I'm loathe to describe her home life critically. The simplest thing I can say is that, like Sarah in Windsor, Jo cares little for housekeeping. She adores her family, and wants them to be happy and healthy. But she sets no store by a well-made bed. She isn't fussed about keeping muddy boots outside, or dogs on the backseat of the car. For Jo, these things just don't matter. When she showed me the room where Paul and I were to sleep, my first thought was that I'd find it easier to fall asleep there if we didn't turn on the light before bed.

Next morning I went out for a walk, stunned by the beauty all around me. I'd forgotten how much I love the English landscape. Muted colours under a grey sky, dark clods of soil underfoot. Walking along, I was soon lost in thought. Jo seemed at home in her farmhouse by the river, as if she'd always lived there. At least from the outside, her life as an artist and mother appeared more seamless than my own. Had I sacrificed something deeper than quality of life by returning to Australia, some kind of earthy maturity that might have emerged from my work and friendships in the UK, and of raising my family amidst that? I would never know. Were I to make the decision again, it would be the same. Still, a yearning for my old life remained.

I hadn't gone far along a muddy path when I saw that, without rubber boots, I couldn't get further along the river path. Entering the kitchen in my socks, in search of rubber boots, I found Jo reading the Sunday paper. Her feet were perched on the rungs of an adjacent chair, next to a wood-burning stove. A puppy was gnawing at one leg of her chair while, nearby, one of her boys was slathering peanut butter on bread. Jo was sitting with her head down reading. She wasn't trying to make sense of her life with a bracing walk, as I was. She wasn't planning her next book, as Paul was. She wasn't finishing a film review before lunch, as her husband was. She looked content to be passing the time in peace. I envied her.

Returning from my walk, I was greeted by the smell of roast lamb and potatoes. Jo was pressing a roll of pastry into a flan tin, her dark hair curtaining her face. I threw a cloth over the table and the four kids were called in for lunch. Lunch was generous: lamb; dumplings; and three vegetables, and everyone seemed glad to be there. After we'd demolished an apple tart, the kids pushed back their chairs and ran into the garden.

The adults remained at the table, sipping coffee and wine. 'You know', said Jo, 'there was once a time when it seemed that I'd never get back into painting.'

'Really?' I said. 'That seems hard to believe.'

'Yes', she said. 'It was just before you left London, when I had that studio in East London. Twice a week, I dropped Louis off at childcare and caught the train out to the studio. When I got there, I'd sit in front of the primus stove, drink coffee and chat to other artists. Some days I'd sit there chatting long enough for someone else to arrive. And so I'd chat to them too. I hardly ever picked up a brush. Eventually, a friend recommended that I see a therapist. "My life is a mess," I blurted out to the therapist in the first session. "I want to paint, but I can't focus. My husband complains that I neglect our flat. And he's right, I do. I just don't care about it. I love my son and I want to have lots more children. But my life isn't working. I can't seem to devote myself to anything." "Look," said the therapist, "it's simple. You're an artist, not a housewife."'

These nine words set Jo free. Whenever she got the chance, she took the train out to her studio then came home to a messy house and left it that way. And because she was happy, her family life chugged along. When the family left London for Essex, she felt even freer now she had a studio fifteen steps from her back door. Propped along the walls of a shed she had insulated herself, sat scores of canvases. The fridge in the kitchen looked bare to me. Yet Jo's heart was full and guests a constant stream. Three days a week, she held painting classes for people who were drawn to paint as much through bewilderment at the pace of life, as through any creative urge. The therapist was right, Jo was an artist.

I admired Jo's disregard for housekeeping. However I knew myself well enough to know that I couldn't escape three unmade beds and muesli stuck to breakfast bowls just by walking out the door each morning. And it wasn't just because I wasn't an artist. I had an imaginative investment in a well-run home. It was part of my creative outlet, my identity even. I liked entering our kitchen, hungry for the next meal, without meeting a sink of dirty dishes. I appreciated it when the cannellini beans in a winter soup were home-cooked, when rosemary flavoured the chicken stock, and when our just-mopped back room glowed in the afternoon light. Jo and I both looked for beauty. But I found it in my home rather than a studio.

I thought a lot about the value of housekeeping before I visited Anita and Jo. But I hadn't embraced it in my heart. On our return to Melbourne, it still unsettled me. But something fundamental had shifted. A tension that had simmered inside me, since having children, was gone. I now felt that my efforts at home were worth making. More than that, I recognised that they were an important part of who I was.

8. creative arts

My eldest aunt once called herself an artist. She spent most of her life on a farm, feeding stock, paying accounts and phoning the vet. Even so, painting and sketching were an important part of her sense of self. She exhibited in group shows and sold paintings through galleries. On holiday, she sat and sketched while her husband packed up camp, or the kettle boiled on the coals. But then, in her mid-60s, when she and my uncle sold their farm and moved to town, she stopped painting. When anyone asked her why, she said that she wanted to stop while she was ahead. 'Besides', she said, 'my eyes aren't what they used to be.' But there was a deeper reason which, on pressing her, she confided to me. She stopped painting, Mary told me, because she was tired of feeling that her work wasn't good enough. I replied that I understood her thinking. Even so, I felt disappointed, let down. Why had she given up the thing she felt most passionate about? What did it matter if her work didn't grace a public gallery? Wasn't it enough that she found it rewarding and that her paintings found buyers outside of a tough gallery system?

On returning to Melbourne, I thought about Mary a lot. One afternoon, as I was tipping a barrow load of compost on to a garden bed, it struck me that my disappointment in Mary was a reflection of my own creative doubts. Like my aunt, I worried that my drawings weren't good enough, that my pies sank in the middle, and that my vision for a creative life would never come to pass because I lacked the follow through to realise it. Like Mary, I struggled to prioritise my creativity in the face of more pressing demands. Too often the sun would set before I got around to doing those things that made my spirit sing. Instead I let myself be waylaid by more urgent-seeming tasks: exercise; laundry; cooking; and kids' schoolwork. I gave myself reasons that were really excuses for not engaging in activities that, everything being equal, which they never were, I enjoyed doing. Instead I grabbed the car keys, took the kids for a walk or flicked open a screen.

From Monday through Friday, I longed for the weekend. I longed for the focus, the uninterrupted hours, the break from daily demands. The weekend promised a window of time in which I could do things I loved doing – drawing, playing piano, sewing, gardening – rather than things I had to do – admin, work deadlines, laundry and vacuuming. But then the weekend would come around and those two precious days slipped through my fingers. One minute they were there, shining with possibility. The next they were gone, the gate of Sunday night clicking shut behind them.

Weekdays had their own rhythm. During school hours, on days I wasn't teaching, I made it a habit to start my writing outside the house, in a café or at a picnic table where housekeeping couldn't reach me. At night, I could only think clearly at my desk once the dinner dishes were done and my kids were tucked up in bed. Too often, I missed out on things that I liked doing at home because I was striving to stay on top of its running. Household tasks took more out of me than I liked to admit. Each night, I underestimated how much energy I needed just to put dinner on the table. Cleaning the oven and unblocking gutters took a certain amount of courage, and I only had finite amounts of it.

Jo and Anita showed me that it takes pluck, not just time, to give myself over to creativity at home. Spending time with them inspired me to set up my life so that my creative side didn't get lost. Being in another hemisphere, even for six weeks, made it clear to me that however overwhelming I found family life to be, there would come a time when its hurly burly would be over. And when that time came, and my kids were out of the house, it was my creativity that would be my guide in bringing me back to myself.

Except that I couldn't afford to wait until the house emptied. Making things, drawing things and sewing things were essential to who I was. Planting out seedlings, baking a tart and moving furniture about whispered to me of the value of home. Amid the chaos of an ordinary day, these things made me feel real, defined and competent. So then why didn't I give more time to them? What was I waiting for?

And so, on Sunday afternoons, I started to do a drawing because it was the weekend. On Saturdays I kneaded bread dough in a way that brought me back to myself. And instead of brushing past a climbing Jasmine, I stopped to tuck its stray tendrils into the trellis. Some of these activities were spontaneous. Others demanded a bit of planning. But the main thing was that I no longer treated them as optional, as rewards for when the housework was done.

Chatting about these pleasures to friends, I discovered that I wasn't the only one to feel them. One friend told me about her late-night efforts to perfect orange marmalade. Another mentioned how much she looked forward to her Monday evening sewing group. A neighbour spent way too much time trawling through the photos on her computer with a view to making a family album. A work colleague started a worm farm and marveled at the fertilising 'tea' it produced. An old school friend spent her annual leave painting each room of her apartment a different colour. And a colleague who'd never cooked for more than four people, threw a dinner for ten. And all of us spent more time in hardware stores than specialist shops. Not everyone I knew had found ways to express themselves creatively at home. But a surprising number had.

Now and then Paul and I invited friends around for Sunday lunch. On Saturday morning, I'd visit the farmers market with a basket in hand and a loose menu in mind. That afternoon, I might make a lasagne or chicken soup which went into the fridge for the next day. I did whatever preparation I could, so that when the doorbell rang I could sit down and relax, confident that what friends wanted, more than lavish food, was a chilled host.

When Anita died three months later, and her ashes were scattered in a field near the Sussex coast, I threw a small lunch without telling the friends I'd invited why. Somehow it felt like the right thing to do. I roasted a chicken the way that Anita taught me, sitting it upside down for half the cooking time before flipping it over to cook evenly. I made her apple tart with vanilla whipped into the cream. And I warmed the pot before making tea as if this really mattered.

ᥣ

Some weeks later, as I traipsed after my kids at the local library, I happened on a section of books about the home. There was shelf after shelf of how-to manuals: how to clean organically; how to upholster a chair; how to prune fruit trees. I took out several of these. At home, sitting with a cup of tea, these books weren't without interest. I learned that wiping a cut potato across the inside of the windscreen stops it fogging up in the cold. I learned that a jam lid of beer drowns slugs. Yet none of these books answered the question that led me to check them out in the first place. Why, I wanted to know, was feeling at home such a subtle yet powerful feeling? And why was achieving it always more challenging than knitting a chunky throw for the end of your bed?

Returning my first pile of books, I exchanged them for ones by Mrs Beeton, Shannon Lush, Cheryl Mendelson and Marie Kondo, reserving others by William Morris, Martha Stewart, Ingegerd Raman, Nigella Lawson and Samin Nosrat. I hoped that these books might expand my sense of what a home could be, that they might show me how to create a home that gave back. But even after leafing through these books, I came up short. Perhaps, I decided, what I was seeking wasn't to be found in any book. I discovered more from an afternoon spent baking with a friend, than from slavishly following a pastry recipe. I lacked knowledge, certainly. But it wasn't ignorance that held me back. It was a subtle form of intimidation. It was shyness that stopped me from trying my hand at domestic arts that I wasn't especially good at.

For years, I'd toyed with the idea of buying a sewing machine. But I always talked myself out of it. A sewing machine symbolised a homeyness that I was attracted to yet wary of. Then there was also the expense of a machine and the awkwardness of storing it. Until, one hot afternoon, lured by a sale at a sewing shop, I finally bought a machine of my own.

I was standing at the counter, waiting to be served, daydreaming about the projects I could tackle and the repairs I could save on, when an older woman, wearing a red jacket I decided she'd sewn herself, approached me.

'Congratulations', she said, beaming. 'It will give you so much pleasure. It has me.'

'Thank you', I said, 'I'm taking it up after a long gap.'

'Why not take a class?' she said. 'You'll learn so much quicker if you do.'

For three weeks my sewing machine sat in the bottom of my study cupboard, zipped up in its plastic hood. By the time I freed it from its case, I'd forgotten how to assemble the bobbin, which meant a trip back to the sewing shop. By which point I accepted that if I was to progress beyond easy-sew patterns, I needed some instruction.

The evening classes I attended were taught by Celia, a sewing teacher for thirty years. Celia called me 'girl', set homework I never did, and made me spend a lesson unpicking everything I'd spent the previous lesson sewing. All the girlfriends I mentioned these classes to had the same response. After looking at me curiously, they said something like, I'd love to do that, but I really don't have time for it. A few looked into the middle distance, as if, were their world were put together differently, with less things in it, they too might find time to sew.

The hours flew by at sewing class. After tracing my skirt pattern onto tissue paper and cutting out the pieces, I marked the notches with a washable pen. Next I pinned, sewed and trimmed the seams, before ironing facing fabric on to the waistband. Working alongside Celia helped me to soak up some of the experience and wisdom so imbued in her that she was unaware of how valuable a novice like me might find them. With just three other women in the class, I could ask as many questions as I liked. Putting in an invisible zip with Celia at my side felt much less stressful than cutting into expensive fabric at home with just a video clip to guide me. When it came to fitting the skirt, Celia took over, pinning it deftly as I scooped up my top and held my tummy in. Making sure not to go off task by checking my phone, I kept my focus until the class was over. Even in a three-hour class, I rarely got as much done as I hoped I might. This was one of the lessons I took away with me. Sewing, like anything creative, assumed an investment of time and energy.

Thanks to these classes, I fell back in love with sewing. I loved cutting with sharp scissors into fabric I'd chosen myself. I loved the crinkle of pattern pieces pinned onto fabric. Most of all, I liked wearing garments fitted to my own body. The measurement from belly button to pelvis, I learned, is different for everyone. And it wasn't until I fitted a pair of pyjamas on myself that I realised I'd spent my life wearing pyjamas that didn't fit. Most of all, I got a buzz out of sewing, from seeing a garment go from start to finish inside a few hours. I got something from my struggle to master it, even knowing I might never arrive. Attending these classes opened me to experiences that my work life didn't always provide. Things as large and hard to pin down as interest, rest and meaning. I also enjoyed working alongside women I mightn't otherwise meet. Sometimes I'd catch myself wondering what community really meant. Then I'd go along to sewing class and feel it as soon as I walked through the door.

In the same way that I'd always wanted to sew, for as long as I could remember I'd wanted to make my own bread. I was fed up rushing to the corner shop, minutes before closing, to buy fluffy plastic-wrapped loaves. I liked the idea of storing flour in a cloth sack. And I delighted in the smell of bread in the oven, instantly turning our house into a home.

So I signed up for a weekend workshop with a baker in the country, arriving with just minutes to spare. Tall, pale and lean, Graham started by introducing his six students to the bakery. Then he turned the focus to himself.

'During my student days', he said, 'I worked in a lot of bakeries. After my partner and I had our first child, we hatched the idea of opening a bakery in a town that was cool enough to prove bread all year round, with its own mill to thresh grain from local growers.'

'Right', he said, interrupting himself, 'let's get down to business. How many of you have made bread before?' Six hands went up.

'How many of you are confident bakers?' No hands went up. 'Okay, let's fix that.' First he took us through the opening moves. 'There is no right way to mix dough. You can mix all the ingredients in a bowl. Or you can mix the water and salt separately before adding them to the flour. It doesn't really matter.' Bother, I thought, wanting an easy answer to the sourdough bricks I'd been baking at home.

'A loaf of bread never lies', Graham continued. 'When you take it from the oven and turn it upside down, a happy loaf makes a duhh-duhh sound when tapped with a spoon. Like this.' He took a loaf in his hand, flipped it over and tapped it.

After watching Graham mix, stretch and shape a few pockets of dough, it was our turn. Eyes glued to the bench, I slapped, folded and quarter-turned my dough, keeping it seam-side down without breaking the skin. But the more I tried, the more a pocket of dough escaped me. An hour passed, which could have been two. Standing at the stainless-steel bench, I felt eight years old. Graham made mixing dough look as simple as making a mud pie. But for me, it felt like fitting a pacemaker.

'Stretch the dough away from you, before rolling it tight and dropping it into a tin. Easy', Graham said, flicking the dough ball off his long fingers into an oiled tin. Frowning, I mentally rehearsed the steps. Slap the dough on the bench. Fold it without breaking the skin, keeping the seam-side down. Repeat till floppy, before rolling it like a nappy and tipping it into an oiled tin. But it was no good. I just couldn't do it.

It takes thousands of hours to master a craft. However it wasn't just inexperience that I was up against that day. I felt uptight, painfully conscious of the hours racing by and the family arrangements I'd made to be there. I just couldn't relax and turn a lump of sticky flour into a warm pouch of dough. Sometime between noon and lunch, I gave up trying to get it right. Graham's son joined us at the bench, and we chatted as we worked. This did the trick. Without even noticing, I started to shape the dough. Not as Graham had shown us, but as his son, with a softer touch, showed me.

'Guys', broke in Graham, just as I was getting the hang of it, 'it's time to see the mill.' I felt disappointed, worried that my progress would be put on hold. Graham ushered us out of the bakery and up a cobbled lane to the newly restored mill where we climbed steep wooden steps to the fourth floor. As we looked out, white canvas sails rushed past the window. No creaking, just an audible whirring. The fact of those sails, turning in the wind to make stone-ground flour, seemed a wonder.

As the afternoon slid into evening, the bakery's wood-fired oven died down enough to take our loaves. Chopped celery and grated cheese were added to half the loaves, pitted olives to a quarter, and soaked dried fruit to the rest. For the first time that day, Graham looked relaxed. Relieved, perhaps, that his apprentices had turned out to be more of a help than a hindrance. And when my loaves came out of the oven, they could barely be told apart from Graham's – a small astonishment to me.

That night at home, I fed my sourdough starter as instructed. Next morning, a Sunday, I got out my earthenware bowl, did up my apron and measured out the ingredients. But it was no good. I just couldn't get the mixture to bind. Was the kitchen too cold? Did the flour need more gluten? Had I soaked too many linseeds? Refusing to admit defeat, I put the dough into the oven anyway, hoping that the heat of the oven would work a miracle. But when I pulled two bricks from the oven, I disappointed my family and embarrassed myself.

It was the same the next time. Thankfully, a few good loaves appeared in between the bricks, enough to make me realise that if I stuck at it I'd work it out. One afternoon, I had a light-bulb moment. After absent-mindedly getting the rising times wrong, I noticed that the loaves that came out didn't suffer my mistake. They were happy loaves that made a duh-duh sound when tapped with a spoon. So perhaps I didn't need to be a slave to fermenting times. Perhaps I could treat baking in the same way that my aunt Mary had done, as a task alongside others, like feeding animals and hanging up washing. I could treat making bread as part of my home work, rather than a lifestyle activity. I could adapt it to the life that I was actually living and leave Graham's baking notes in the cupboard. I could bake less like a baker and more like myself, a busy woman running a family home.

So it was. After arriving at a few rules, I let baking fall in with my actual life, rather than the one I fantasised living. My loaves often came out of the oven on the sour side, with a harder crust than the ones at the bakery. Even so, they made great toast for breakfast, or topped with a boiled egg and greens for lunch. And they were a wonderful gift for friends, wrapped in a tea-towel, warm from the oven.

All the same, I understood why more people didn't make their own bread. Good flour isn't cheap, busy lives don't synch with rising times, sourdough starters need regular feeding, and scrubbing wet flour from your fingers is, well, yuk. However, once I got into baking, these felt like minor hassles. The real challenge went deeper. Each time I tied up my apron and threw a cloth across the table, I felt a flash of hopelessness. As I measured out the ingredients: 200 grams of sourdough starter mixed with filtered water in a jug; 1kg of sifted mixed flours; 2 teaspoons of salt; a quarter cup of linseeds dissolved in half a cup of boiling water; and depending on the strength of the flour, a tablespoon or two of gluten, I didn't feel confident. Staring into my earthenware bowl, I saw a mixture that resembled the muck from my kids' sandpit. Could this sticky mess come together to form a dough that I could throw and shape?

Each time I stood before my big blue bowl, I felt this moment of despair. And it was only replaced with a small burst of pride when the dough took on an airy shape like a baby's bottom. I may have to add water or flour to the mix. I may have to be more patient than I naturally was. But eventually, the dough always did that amazing thing which bakers call binding, when the strands of gluten in the flour relaxed enough for the mixture to form an elastic dough.

When a close friend asked me for tips on how to bake bread, I laughed and suggested that she take a class. 'It doesn't matter whether or not you learn from a master baker', I said. 'But it does help to get through the early steps in good company. Think back to how you felt on learning to tie your own shoelaces. Making bread, at the outset, reduces you to the same level of clumsiness. It's a skill that, weirdly tricky at the start, takes time to become second nature. And it helps, during this clumsy stage, to have someone at your side who can reassure you and help you to see the funny side. With a baker at your side, you can banish the taunting voice in your head that tells you that you'll never get the hang of it. Until, one day, the magic will happen and you'll be making your own bread.'

CB

On the shelf in the pantry, sat eight cookbooks. Now and then I'd pick one out and flick through it. But more to confirm a hunch or adapt a recipe than for detailed instruction. I already knew how to cook a perfectly good lasagne, I told myself, as I glanced through a cookbook standing up. I'd never guess ingredients when it came to baking, but I rarely consulted a cookbook before the evening meal.

Family and friends thought that I could cook quite well. But I always felt that I was making it up as I went along. Week in, week out, I cooked family-friendly dishes: fish fingers; bolognese sauce; fish croquettes; casserole and risotto. I did this for a few reasons: to avoid shopping for special ingredients; to overcome my resentment at the constancy of family cooking; and for the sheer ease of it. Besides, I was never just cooking when I was in the kitchen. I was returning texts on my phone, listening out for the beep-beep of the washing machine in the basement and, not least, keeping an eye on the emotional temperature of whomever happened to be at home.

One afternoon, I bought myself a new cookbook, a big illustrated hardback called *What to Cook and How to Cook It* by Jane Hornby. Returning home with it under my arm I felt confident that, if anything could cajole my family into joining me at the chopping board, it was this book. With it as a guide, the evening meal would be a joint venture. The step-by-step photos were so appealing that I felt sure that it was just a matter of time before I was upstaged in the kitchen. Alongside a list of ingredients for chicken pie, say, was a photo of a leek, two carrots, a spoonful of thyme leaves, two garlic cloves, two chicken breasts, a jug of cream, puff pastry, a rolling pin and a pinch of salt, all laid out on a table like surgical instruments before an operation.

That evening, with some excitement, I showed the book to Paul and our kids. Alex was nearing the top of primary school, and a few of his friends were cooking family meals. For two long weeks after, the new cookbook sat untouched, virginal, on the windowsill. When I finally opened it, sulkily as I hadn't bought it for myself, I was immediately reminded of why I'd bought it. It was a cookbook aimed at people like me who winged it in the kitchen. It was for people who thought that they knew how to stir fry beef and assemble a fish pie without being shown how. For people who thought they were above being shown how to cook dishes that they'd never been instructed in.

Cooking with this book at my side felt like having a trusted friend in the kitchen. Page after page showed me how to cook in a way that I'd secretly hoped someone might. The step-by-step photos forced me to slow down. Usually, for example, I blitzed all the ingredients for Pesto sauce into a fluffy paste. Now that I knew better, I dropped the grated Parmesan into the food processor at the end and pulsed the ingredients ever so lightly. I mixed flour and water into casseroles towards the end of cooking, rather than earlier on. I left a gap between the pie filling and the pastry, using an upturned eggcup to stop the pastry going soggy in the middle. With this book for company I started looking forward to meals rather than wishing them away. Using it inspired me to pull other cookbooks from the shelf and to drop oil on their pages.

Eventually Emma, who looked on cooking as a chore akin to school homework, suggested that we might cook something from 'that book.' Because she did most of her homework at the kitchen table, she was wise to my struggles in the kitchen. She knew all about it when I burned a favourite pan dry. She spied me cutting corners when dinner was late. She heard me swear when something went wrong. And my triumphs? Well, mostly she took these for granted. And because she saw me treat cooking as a chore, she held back from joining me at the kitchen bench. She'd bake a cake when the mood took her. But she wouldn't muck in, as her brother did, when things heated up before dinner. So the idea that she might actually want to cook with me meant a lot.

One Saturday, round this time, a neighbour of ours invited us for brunch. It was a proud moment for Di, who was opening her home to a university friend who she'd met long before a home of her own had seemed desirable or even possible. When we arrived, Di wasn't sitting smugly in her newly-painted scarlet living room. She was busy in the kitchen, getting scrambled eggs on the table before the plates got cold. As I helped Di serve the eggs, her friend put her head around the kitchen door. 'Di, why can't you just relax and be as you used to be? What does it matter if there are chives in the eggs? I hate you being busy out here.' Without looking up from the plates, Di gave a little stamp. 'I'll relax when the food is on the table', she said. 'Cold eggs are horrid.'

It would have been easy to side with Di's old friend. But I knew that Di's love of domesticity was no pose. I knew that she'd been raised by a father who brought her up single-handed in the country, that she'd cooked from an early age, and that she longed to create the kind of childhood for her kids that she hadn't enjoyed. So I didn't feel sorry for Di. I admired her. Whether it was scrambled eggs on the weekend, or lamb shanks on a school night, her meals seemed like small triumphs to me.

When I was a girl, I often wondered why my mother, a perfectly good home cook, used to fuss whenever she cooked for more than family. Entertaining seemed to wear her out, rather than replenish her. Was this why, as she grew older, she came to avoid it? Growing up, I often wished that she entertained more, because I liked it when people were gathered together. Until, that is, I had a family of my own and, in the hour before friends were due to arrive, I'd be feeling frazzled, on the edge of wishing they weren't coming. I'd be cooking my kids' dinner, blending soup, filling school lunch boxes and hoping that there'd be time to change out of my jeans before the doorbell rang. If one of our guests happened to be a good cook or a chef, I fretted even more. I imagined they had cooking techniques at their fingertips I knew nothing of. Sauce tricks and braising methods that were like Braille to me. They weren't beset by the errant thoughts that raced through my mind as I chopped vegetables and laid the table, thoughts which didn't stop until I was reduced to feeling like a part-time writer, part-time housekeeper, part-time mother, part-time wife: part-time me.

Every year, on Paul's birthday, we invited friends for dinner. Over the years, this became my present to him. Unusually for me, on this particular birthday I set the table for dinner well before the guests arrived. By the time there was a knock at the door, I was feeling stressed. Still, it was a relief to greet real people, rather than the imaginary guests I'd been carrying in my head as I washed up my kids' dinner plates. When 8pm passed and Paul, who was teaching late, still hadn't appeared, seven of us sat down to eat a beef dish that I'd prepared the night before. Just then, Paul's key turned in the front door. Seconds later, his face peered round the living room door with four smiling students behind him.

'We had a drink after class', Paul said, grinning. 'And I thought that, since it was my birthday, a few more would be welcome.'

'Of course', I said, my heart missing a beat as we shuffled the place settings and I ladled the pasta dish a little less generously. I stared at Paul, who smiled back.

'You know', piped a young Brazilian student who I was meeting for the first time, 'I really miss sitting down at a big table like this. My mother thought nothing of cooking for fifteen people when I was growing up in Sao Paulo.'

'And what about you?' I asked. 'Do you like cooking for friends?'

'Oh no', she laughed, 'I'm way too disorganised. Besides I can barely cook. But I'm sure that one day I will.'

After the hiccup of late arrivals, the evening mellowed. But I never forgot the feeling of Paul springing four extra guests on me. Making others feel at home around our table was a grace that didn't come naturally to me. But with practice, I was gaining it.

Over the years, two tricks helped me to overcome the jangly nerves that often beset me when I cooked for friends. First, it seemed to work best when I prepared the main dish ahead of time, ideally the night before. My other salve was to keep things simple, confident that none of my friends would want me to slave in the kitchen on their behalf. These tricks helped me to focus on what really mattered, which was getting to know friends better around the table. It was never just about food. It was also about love.

Far from shrinking my horizons, the domestic arts were expanding them, offering me quiet salvation in a stressful world. Being passionate about cooking, baking and growing things helped me to feel less driven, more positive about life as a whole. I loved spying seedlings poking up by the back door. Slapping down bread dough on the kitchen bench felt physical, yet restful too. I loved passing through the kitchen to the smell of something cooking. And I knew that I wasn't wasting my time on this earth when, on a busy weekend, I could pull two plump loaves from the oven. Unlike juggling household accounts, or clearing cupboards, domestic creativity offered its own reward.

From the outside, domestic satisfactions like cooking and gardening were simple pleasures. But in my experience, they were never easy pleasures. They weren't like reading a book or going for a walk. They didn't just happen. They assumed a bit of psychological know-how and planning. It wasn't enough for me just to talk about making an apple pie on the weekend. If I wanted to actually make a pie crust, I needed the right flour in the cupboard. I needed to carve out time on a busy Saturday morning to blind bake it. I needed, in other words, to make it a priority. And if the pie didn't work out, I needed to laugh it off and to try again another time. Baking assumed practice and patience. And like other life skills, grit.

Visiting farmer's markets, playing the piano, making bread and sewing the basics made our house feel like home to me. Realising this, accepting this, changed everything. Because if this was what I really cared about, what were we doing living on the edge of another big city? Wouldn't it be better to live in a smaller city, with a slower pace and nature on the doorstep, somewhere where our kids could wander off and make their own discoveries, leaving Paul and me to get on with what was important to us?

So it was. We would stop trying to make it in Melbourne, which had come to feel increasingly like London with its commercial and professional pressures. Money was tight in this expensive city and, with my kids nearing secondary school, I sensed a growing pressure to get a proper job. Meanwhile the pull to write, which I couldn't rely on for income, was as strong as ever.

The answer? A tree change. On the strength of a holiday to Tasmania, we started looking for a house at the bottom of Australia that might match our hopes and dreams. I didn't need much persuading. I loved the state's towering coasts and vast national parks. Both our kids were learning to sail, and were drawn to the idea of living on an island. Paul, an urbanite, was attracted to the old buildings and unspoiled feel of the cities. As a family, it was a desire to live more simply. But also more ambitiously. It was a longing to live somewhere cooler than Melbourne, with fewer people and less expectation to be a certain way. I loved our house in Melbourne. But I knew that it wasn't the only house I could love. Opportunity was knocking, and we decided to open the door.

9. renovating

It was a cold May morning and the four of us were standing outside a house in Hobart that we'd arranged to inspect. The real estate agent texted that he was running late and that we were welcome to look around the garden. 'Arden 1852', said a copper plate on the wooden gate, which squeaked on its hinges. Alex and Emma raced ahead to see who could get to the bottom of the garden first. The rain overnight had been heavy, causing the camellias in the front garden to hang face down, sodden. When Paul and the kids disappeared round the back, I stayed behind, gazing up at the peeling window frames with their twelve wafer-thin panes of glass. A drain pipe hung askew and, all around, the garden was a jungle of damp, overgrown trees. How, I wondered, had our small London flat led us to the overgrown driveway of this beautiful, daunting house?

The kids returned, panting. 'We couldn't find the bottom of the garden', Alex said. 'It just keeps on going.' Laughing, I followed them round the back. Alex disappeared into what looked like a secret hideout, a garden shed covered in matted vines. Emma threw bits of gravel into a bird bath shrouded by weeds. I was halfway down the grass, when Alex joined me. 'Hurry up', he said excitedly, 'we're not there yet.' Alex was right, the fence at the bottom of the garden was obscured by a thicket of brambles and a pineapple vine gone mad. Paul saw nothing but potential in the house. What looked like peeling window frames and dangling downpipes to me translated into faded grandeur for him.

When the agent arrived, we joined him in the driveway. 'The previous owners', he explained, looking up at the house, 'let this place go at the end of their time here. Which means that whoever takes on this property', he said silkily, 'is in for a big job.'

Inside, the musty carpet smelled of dog. Textured wallpaper dangled like carrot peel in the living room and the upstairs hallway. The basement lacked a proper floor and housed a dentist's chair, a small stage and half a row of theatre seating. Weeds rioted on three sides of the garden. And all that remained of the rose garden, a highlight of the real estate brochure, was rocks and stumps. It was a place of lost dreams.

As overwhelmed as I felt, there was no mistaking the grand bones of the building. It had aspects of every National Trust house I'd ever visited, only without the restoration – and team of volunteers – to rescue it. And beneath the wear and tear, a family home shone through. It was the kind of home I'd grown up in myself.

Breaking into my daydream, the real estate agent handed me a sepia photo of the facade of the house in its early days. A couple in their Sunday best were silhouetted against the newly plastered façade. The man was wearing a top hat while the woman, a bonnet shading her face, nursed a baby in a wicker chair. I passed over to Paul the grainy image.

'Hey', Paul said. 'Look at that terrace. And the facade looks so pristine, as if they finished painting it yesterday.'

Looking out at the garden, the terrace of which was now the neighbour's house, I made myself a promise. We could only take on a house this old, this much in need of work, if I was willing to work on it myself. I felt excited, cocky even. But also humble. Paul and I renovated well together. But we'd never taken on a project this big. If we put our hand up for this house, it would change us all.

With hearts in our mouths, we put in an offer which was accepted. A few days later, the sale was done. Selling our house in Melbourne, and packing it up, took longer. I found saying goodbye to friends especially painful. It felt like another betrayal, just as leaving London had been. Yet I didn't waver. I wanted this move, with its promise of a different kind of life, a gentler one, for us all.

Within a few weeks of moving in to our big old house, Paul set up to work remotely. Meanwhile I put aside nine months to renovate, treating it as a job, along with settling our kids into a new school and city. The floors were my first task. Scraping the wide floorboards by hand, sanding them with steel wool before staining and varnishing them, gave me plenty of time to think. (Getting a professional sander in wasn't possible as we were living in the house.) Working with my hands away from my desk left me feeling freer than I had in years. Whole sequences of my past life flashed through my mind. The buses I'd taken through London to various publishing jobs, the flats I'd lived in north and south of the river, the flatmates I'd shared them with, the novels I'd taught and the students I'd befriended. A life that had been mine, back when thoughts about family were the blink of an eye, streamed through my mind.

What was the name of that lovely girl I made friends with in that Soho restaurant I first worked in? Which temping job, I wondered, yanking a square convict nail from a floorboard, had I taken the number 28 bus through Pimlico to? It wasn't just facts that I was tracking down. Sights and smells from a world I'd left behind rose up as I worked. Was it nostalgia that I felt for the scent of thyme on the windowsill of my first flat? Perhaps. Certainly, it was chastening to realise how much of my past had been gobbled up by my present. I hadn't forgotten these memories, exactly. I just hadn't been in the right frame of mind – loose, open, meditative – to entertain them. Why, I asked myself, was I always rushing towards something, when there was so much to learn from what I'd left behind?

Renovating an old house in a new city is scary. The financial outlay and effort involved isn't for the faint-hearted. I took to it with relish. Wearing a white t-shirt, dungarees and runners, I painted walls and treated floors, scooted furniture from room to room on a blanket, working so steadily, often skipping lunch, that I arrived at the school gates for pick up a little late. I bought bathroom taps and a basin from the recycling shop, and persuaded the plumber to connect a bath with claws, which no sensible person would expect to be carried round the hairpin bend at the top of our stairs. But the carpenter, plumber and handyman accomplished the task with much groaning.

New friends admired my tenacity. However what they couldn't see was how liberating it was to be able to focus on just one thing. Released from both paid work and motherhood, during the blessed school hours, I was able to catch up with myself, following the breadcrumbs of my passing thoughts. Freedom was something I'd been hungering for in this move. Still, I was surprised by the depth of the transformation. Had I arrived? Or was this the start of a new chapter that would end, just like previous ones had? In my heart, the move felt permanent, as serious and exciting as getting married had felt.

The sepia photo that the real estate agent gave us when the sale went through laid the ground for everything Paul and I struggled with as we renovated. I loved the jungly garden, camellias competing with vines and saplings growing any which way, as on a forest floor. Paul loved the house for its strong bones, and for what the garden could be if it were cleared and returned to its early glory.

Rather than bringing in an architect, we relied on Paul's design sense, along with the ingenuity of a local builder and handyman for whom no challenge was too great. An architecture drop-out, Paul retained a vision for the house and solved the day-to-day design problems. He knew immediately that the kitchen was in the wrong room and that the back area, covered with pavers and an asbestos sleep-out, concealed a courtyard that promised to be the heart of the garden. My strengths lay in project-managing, in working alongside tradies, overseeing the finances, painting and decorating, and making sure various 'bits' appeared on time on site. I also made the people who worked for us countless cups of tea, because it seemed like the right thing to do.

Before leaving Melbourne, I visited a homewares store to cost curtains for our new old house. As I fingered expensive linens, I fell into conversation with a Greek sales assistant who was neatening rolls of fabric in the harshly-lit fabric department. When I mentioned that I was renovating an old house, she launched into a detailed explanation of how to make lined curtains.

'It's *so* easy', she said.

I was skeptical. Her description didn't sound easy to me. But what a difference it would make, I thought, in terms of cost, if I could sew my own lined curtains.

'Do you think', I asked, overcoming my shyness, 'that rather than telling me how to make them, you could actually show me?'

'Of course. It would be a pleasure', she said, and bustled off. Two minutes later she returned with two sheets of orange paper, pins, curtain tape and sticky tape. After setting them down on the counter, she picked up the curtain tape, cut it and pinned it to three layers of folded orange paper, folding the top of the bottom orange sheet under the curtain tape pinned at the top. It was a simple task, a minute at most. But for me, watching the sales assistant assemble the mock curtain was a revelation. By the time she'd finished folding, cutting, taping and pinning, fitting the layers of fabric 'like a sandwich' and securing them with tape, I saw with my own eyes how to make a lined curtain. I felt like giving her a hug, but made do with holding her hands and thanking her.

The week after we moved in to our old house, a furnishings lady came around to quote for blinds and curtains, working quietly for the best part of an hour with tape measure, swatches and notepad. The next day, she left a quote on wispy paper in the letterbox, a figure higher than the cost of rewiring the house. Before receiving this quote I doubted that I was up to making curtains. Holding this quote in my hand convinced me that I could.

Paul thought I was mad to make so many curtains. With an expression he has which involves not actually saying anything, he made it clear that most people get a proper job and pay someone else to make curtains. My mother, for her part, sounded worried. 'Aren't lined curtains terribly heavy to hang?' she asked over the phone. 'Mind you don't fall off the ladder!'

Two days later the furnishings lady came back to check the blind measurements. When I told her my plan, she looked up sharply. 'Have you made lined curtains before?' Her brow arched.

'No', I said, 'but I know an easy way how.'

A small snort escaped her. 'Good luck', she said, snapping her card on the hall table. 'Call me when you need me.'

I learned to sew late and patchily, and will never be an accomplished sewer. I regularly curse my machine, moan loudly when the tension is loose and the thread loops drunkenly. My fingers feel like blubber when it's time to reassemble the bobbin. But I'd promised myself that I'd do all the renovating I could do myself, myself. And, thanks to the classes I'd taken, I knew how to sew. Making curtains for a big draughty house was a challenge in line with all the others that renovating had thrown my way. Like all the other domestic arts I'd taken up, I was making it up as I went along. Checking the window measurements one last time, I was learning by doing. Good enough curtains really were, I told myself, good enough. They just had to frame the windows and keep draughts out at night. And if, in a few years' time, we tired of cream curtains, I could always change them.

For a few minutes after the furnishings' lady left, I sat in the sun on the front doorstep. Perhaps, I thought, I really was mad. Then I went inside, picked up my phone and called a fabric wholesaler in Melbourne.

'Three-layered curtains, you say?' the wholesaler asked, chuckling. 'Where are you living, a lighthouse?'

'No. An old unheated house in Hobart.'

'I see', he said. 'In that case, you'll need two rolls of block-out fabric, two more of thermal and the same of calico or canvas.'

'Is that all?' I asked.

'Curtain tape and hooks', he said. 'But you can pick these up once you're underway.' He paused to add up the cost, a satisfying eighty percent less than the furnishing lady's quote. 'But', the wholesaler said, 'for that price, you'll have to pay me online before I courier the fabrics to you.' He agreed to send samples by post, and I agreed to get back to him that week.

Ten days later, after the samples had arrived and I had paid him, the bolts of fabric arrived on our porch. I took a deep breath, dragged them inside, fetched the mock curtain the sales assistant had made me, made a mug of tea and set to work. If I hadn't had that mock paper curtain I wouldn't have known where to begin. In a matter of minutes, the sales assistant had given me the tools and confidence I needed to get on with the job.

After unrolling wide rolls of fabric across the sitting room floor, I crunched scissors into calico on bare floorboards. With music turned up, I was soon caught up sewing. Cutting the fabric proved the easy part. I despaired when the sewing machine played up, or I jabbed my finger on a pin as I sewed curtain tape on to an impossibly fat fabric sandwich. Forcing this wodge of fabric under the foot of my machine led me to sweat and curse. As I worked, a favourite children's picture book came to mind, about a baby penguin forced to march across snow and ice, and of his mother's words to get him started. 'Just take one step', his mother urged, 'and then the next. That's all you have to do.' Like the baby penguin, I focused on the next hem, the next seam, knowing that if I could do that, and only that, the curtains would take care of themselves.

Once done with stitching, I heaved the layers of fabric up the ladder, attached the hooks to the runner with difficulty as my fingers proved too big for the space between the metal runner and wooden pelmet, and held my breath as the fabric turned into a curtain that cascaded from the top of the ladder. As it fell, I crossed my fingers that the length would be right. My first pair of curtains, amazingly, were the perfect length.

Four times out of five, the curtain hem tipped the floor and I breathed a sigh of relief. And when I got the length wrong, I had an easy work-around. After taking the curtain down, I attached more fabric to the hem, telling myself that no-one but me would be the wiser. And bar my sharp-eyed daughter, they weren't. None of my curtains were perfect, and they were far from the linens I'd fantasised using. To tone with the off-white of the walls, the downstairs curtains were canvas, prewashed to soften. Upstairs in the bedrooms, the top layer was calico. And so, just as the sales assistant had assured me, one by one the curtains went up.

There was no more mystery in the art of making curtains than there was in making bread. Making a house into a home required patience, time and focus, plus a willingness to struggle and to take the first step. What a month before had seemed insurmountable was now behind me, giving me the confidence to go on and do other seemingly impossible tasks. And what a difference it made, in terms of warmth and homeyness, to pull curtains across black windows when the evenings drew in and the temperature dropped. Looking round the house, I felt proud that I'd kept out the dark with my own hands.

CS

Dave, our handyman, had rough hands. Yet the pads on his fingers were worn smooth. Whenever he worked with putty, he'd finish it off with a flick of his index finger, as if it were a tool from the hardware store. His clothes were smeared with paint and goo from countless previous jobs. Softly spoken and willing to turn his hand to anything, he thought nothing of his skills: plumbing; roofing; gardening; electrics; carpentry; and decorating. A self-taught builder, who left school at 14, the only skill Dave lacked was self-promotion.

Every morning at 9am, throughout our renovation, Dave knocked lightly at the front door. Rain or shine, sick or well, I could count on his knock. G'day, he'd say, and we'd discuss the morning's work. After an hour or so I'd track him down for another chat, this time with a mug of milky tea and a few biscuits. And again in the afternoon. Sometimes I minded these chats. Why were we passing the time of day chatting, when there were so many jobs to be getting on with? But then slowly I realised that, as in all relationships, everything ran more smoothly when Dave and I shared something of our lives over and above the jobs we were doing.

Working alongside Dave, I learned practical skills: how to lay tiles; prep for painting; mix cement; and plug large holes with it. More than skills, I learned from his example that the most important thing, when renovating, is to get on with jobs as they come up. Rather than wait until everything was on hand for a task, he schooled me to start straight away with what was on hand, and to pick up 'the bits' as I went along.

Towards the end of our renovation, I complained to Dave about the jasmine vine that grew wantonly along the fence from the front door to the gate. Since the day we moved in, this vine had drooped like a line of unmilked cows. Each time I brushed past its heaving rebuke, I wished that it would magically lift itself up. But somehow there were always more urgent things to do than to fix this vine.

'Hang on a minute', Dave said. He headed out to his van and returned with a roll of garden wire, a drill and a pocket full of screws. He instructed me to hold one end of the wire which we strung along the fence in rows like washing line, while he fixed the wire with long screws drilled into the fence. Then he told me to pick up hunks of vine, hook the biggest runners around the screws and tuck loose tendrils under the wire. That was it. Fifteen minutes at most and my wish had come true. And from that day, the vine was young again.

It wasn't just Dave's skills that impressed me. It was his willingness to turn his hand to anything. Or was it, more accurately, his absence of unwillingness? Working alongside Dave helped me to see that it was my dilly-dallying that held me back, as much as my lack of experience.

ɔȝ

For years I was drawn to books on interiors in local libraries. Poring over colours and arrangements, I tried to distinguish beautiful photography from good design. Renovating an old house gave me a chance to put some of the ideas I gleaned from these books into practice. I researched environmentally-friendly paints, trawled second-hand shops and scanned small ads for interesting finds. In the garden, I played with simple, hardy solutions: acanthus; agapanthus; salvias; rosemary; and geraniums. As the weeks galloped by my hands developed calluses just like Dave's. My dungarees lost their stiffness and became blobbed with paint. I felt worn out and also thrilled to have accomplished so much, just by keeping going and getting help when I needed it. The end was in sight and I could almost feel it.

The kitchen was our last big task. On first moving in, my fantasy had been to convert the living room, with its triple bay window, into a kitchen with a wood-burning oven that warmed the whole house. But the high cost and plumbing challenges this posed forced me to give my plan up. Instead we opted for the sensible choice, the back room with its sun-catching window overlooking the courtyard. Even this choice posed plumbing problems. But they were smaller and more doable.

By this point, I'd grown impatient of cooking in a '50s galley kitchen on a hob that we called Big Bertha. Even so, I'd been renovating for long enough to know that I couldn't just wave a wand for the kitchen I longed for to appear. I started by shopping round, and asking after friends' favourite appliances. When it came to the big purchases, a self-cleaning oven topped my list. The sales assistant in the homewares store that I visited seemed friendly and keen.

'What kind of oven are you looking for?' he asked.

When I explained what I wanted, he frowned. 'I think you'll find that the model in your price range with a self-cleaning function is less efficient than the conventional model.'

'Oh', I said, 'I really hate cleaning ovens.'

'Do you?' he asked, looking surprised. 'I find that if I wipe out the oven, straight after cooking, keeping it clean is no big deal.'

'You mean you wipe out the oven every time you use it?'

'Of course', he said. 'It's only lazy people who let their oven get so bad that it's horrible to clean.'

In that second, a gulf opened up between the salesman and myself. I was one of those lazy people who let their oven fill with oils before disgust forced me to clean it. Like so many things in the domestic sphere, an oven wasn't just an oven. In that moment, I decided to pass on choosing an oven and left the showroom. On my way home, sitting at the traffic lights, I had a thought. That salesman, I decided, had no idea what it might be like to serve dinner for a hungry family every night. But, I thought darkly, one day he might.

'Do we really have to have a fridge in the middle of the kitchen, spoiling the space and making that horrible whirring noise that old fridges make?' asked Paul, the night before the plumber and electrician were booked to install the new kitchen. We frowned at each other. I knew what he was saying. He was saying that I should have bought a new fridge, rather than keep the old one that came with the house. 'Why not put the fridge in the pantry?' he said, brightening, as if not having a fridge in the kitchen was a normal thing.

'What pantry?' I asked, knowing full well that what he called the pantry was a damp, foundationless space between the new kitchen and the spare bedroom that the previous owners, for reasons of their own, had painted matt black. 'Won't that mean going up and down six steps every time we need the fridge?'

'What's so bad about that?' said Paul, as he left the kitchen to take a call.

I could think of a few things. I stared out the window at the court-yard below. Paul had given way on so much, in his life with me, not least accompanying me to Australia. Somehow it felt right that I should give way when it came to form over function in the kitchen. And so it was. Next morning, the plumber and electrician installed a sink, range hood, hob and dishwasher, and wheeled the old fridge into the pantry. At this point, all I cared about was having a working kitchen in a sunny room. I'd have agreed to ten steps down to the fridge if it meant eating breakfast in our own bright kitchen.

It took a bit of getting used to having the fridge next to the kitchen. But I never regretted my decision. Despite the inconvenience, Paul was right. It did mean running in and out of the pantry with a tray of ingredients whenever I cooked. But I loved that the room I spent most time in – bar asleep in bed – didn't have a fridge taking up space and making that annoying whirring noise old fridges make.

Having Dave around to keep me company while renovating helped with the hardest part of every job – starting. He showed me that it was the little jobs that made the biggest difference, and that usually these took less time than I thought they might. Importantly, he showed me how to break down messy jobs into steps, even if only to write a note in my diary or to take a photo of an offending gutter, and to eat the elephant that way.

One cold autumn afternoon, our work on the house came to a halt. Dave, the carpenter and I lit the wood-burning stove and had tea in the living room to celebrate. The renovation wasn't finished. Ours was the kind of house that would always be a work in progress. However, we'd hit our budget and I was itching to get back to my desk. We'd done what we set out to do. We'd created a home. Now it was time to live in it.

Dave was no longer a daily presence, but he was still around. He was with me when I avoided a straightforward job like putting putty around loose window panes. He was with me when I moved a plant in the garden, shoveled compost over a hungry flower bed, or divided agapanthus with a spade. He wasn't there to chat to, but he was there, still is, as a guide and prompt.

10. cinderella

I began to write for a local lifestyle magazine. I loved the buzz of the work. I was given unusual freedom to write at length and to interview subjects who fascinated me. A year later, I took over as editor and the work became full-time. There was just one drawback. On returning home, late afternoon, I met dirty dishes in the sink and two piles of laundry, one clean and unfolded, the other bunched up and dirty.

When, two years later, the magazine collapsed, I moved into freelance work. I was at home once more. However being at home wasn't the creative outlet that it had been during our renovations. And I was back to my weekly housekeeping routine. On top of this we'd acquired a rescue puppy whose black hairs flecked the white painted stairs, ridiculing my vacuuming efforts. Some days, clearing up after my kids, I felt myself siding with their unwillingness to see housekeeping as real work. What did it matter whether the house got cleaned? Why, really, did I bother?

Now that Alex and Emma were teenagers, there seemed something elemental about their reluctance to help around the house. They did their job for the day, the one thing we agreed that I could ask of them and that they couldn't refuse for fear of me losing it. But mostly that was it. Just as it had been between my mother and me when I reached the age my kids were now.

Over the years, without my having a say in it, Paul and our kids came to the conclusion that I hated doing housework. However I knew it wasn't that simple. Generally they came across me cleaning the house at the end of the day, when there were already other demands on me. I was frustrated, they were right about that. But it wasn't necessarily the housework that rankled. I'd be vacuuming and dusting the house, making it into a game by trying to finish within the hour. Bang on 4.30pm, Alex would wheel his bike on to the front porch, his helmeted head outlined in the glass panels on either side of the front door. As he dropped the door knocker – he had a key but rarely used it – my domestic bubble burst and I started feeling self-conscious about an activity that, minutes before, absorbed me. Was I demeaning myself by cleaning up after my family? Did I really hate housework? Or was it, more accurately, that I hated having my domestic flow interrupted?

One afternoon, as I was doing up my apron for what I'd come to think of as my afternoon shift, Emma came home, flushed from walking after missing the school bus. Dropping her bag in the hall, she slumped on a stool in the kitchen, where she sat unmoving, flicking through a magazine, wordlessly hoping that a snack might come her way.

'*Would* you pick up your bag, rather than dropping it out here like a sack of potatoes?' I called to her in my mother's sharp tone of voice, one I rarely used. I put away the vacuum cleaner and entered the kitchen, where Emma hadn't moved from her chair.

'Why', I said, 'should I have to care about all these things that I don't give a damn about while you just get to sit there?' With that, I started jabbing at the diced leeks stuck to the bottom of the pan with a wooden spoon.

Emma got up and joined me at the hob. '*Poor* Cinderella', she said, 'has to do all these things she doesn't want to do. Poor Cinderella', she repeated, peering hopefully into the pan. I bit my lip, knowing how quickly I could cut down my daughter. She was, after all, much closer in age to Cinderella than I was. Still, I didn't volley a return. Why not? Well, because in that second, I was in Emma's shoes. So I knew that she hadn't dropped her bag in the hall just to annoy me. I knew that she couldn't begin to imagine what it was like to be responsible for the daily running of a home. And I was certain of this because, years ago that felt like the flick of a switch, I'd been too busy being a teenager to notice how few of the good things in life: clean clothes, regular meals, and watered plants came easily. Just like Emma, I was educated to stand up for myself, and to put my best energies into carving out a niche in the world. Just like her, I'd grown up hoping to leave the world, not my home, a better place.

It wasn't so different with my son. A few days after Emma called me Cinderella, Alex came home tired from sailing and flopped on his bed with a magazine, a packet of breadsticks, a jar of pesto and two apples. Just as he was relaxing, I burst out swearing in the kitchen, loud enough to draw a response. In a flash, Alex vaulted up the pantry steps and put his hand on my shoulder. 'Don't worry', he said, as I tipped burnt rice into a colander. 'You're not really horrible. You just sound it.' Setting the colander down, I took in a sharp breath, and Alex disappeared outside.

The transformation was complete. Housekeeping had worked its own bad magic. Just as I'd feared on that French rooftop all those years ago, I was, in my kids' eyes, a small-minded, snarly housewife. Leaning against the kitchen bench, arms folded, I gazed out the window. Alex was hosing down his bike, picking up the seat and spinning the back wheel. And I was in the kitchen swimming in a problem that I couldn't fix. Because it wasn't just my kids who didn't credit the time and energy that I put into housekeeping. Friends and relatives gave me more credit for the time that I spent writing and renovating, than for the quarter of each day that I spent on home work.

I turned away from the window and went back to the dishes in the sink. Should I jump up and down and shout my frustration, slamming cupboard doors as my mother once did? Should I force my time-poor family into a fair share of household tasks? I turned back to the window. Noticing my stare, Alex looked up, dropped the seat of his bike and smiled. I smiled back. And I knew, in that second, that my frustration wasn't his fault. It was the domestic order of things that I was protesting against. I was railing against having to care about a whole raft of things that I didn't really care about, from potatoes to socks to utility bills. And it was this that led me to feel weak and put upon at the exact same moment that my kids came through the door, their energy low after a long day.

I sank down into a squat, my back against the dishwasher. Surely, I asked myself, there must be another way. I knew that my housekeeping days for a family of four were numbered. And that, when they were over, I would feel relieved but also sad. Knowing this, wasn't there a way of bypassing resentment and of taking a kinder, more Zen-like view of the many tentacled octopus that housekeeping had become for me? What if, instead of making a fuss, I just kept on keeping on, and took pride in doing so?

Family life, in my experience, was nothing like the world beyond the front door. It wasn't shaped by outcomes, the bottom line or social status. Just as it had been for my mother, it was about keeping the trains running on time. With two teenagers, a writer husband and a rescue dog in the house, unless I wanted to end each day shouting, family life was about yielding and bending and biting my lip. It wasn't about being right or arguing my corner. I would never be in a position to demand a pay rise or Sundays off. And this situation was no-one's fault. It just was.

My kids weren't especially mean or selfish. I knew that they loved and cared for me. It was more that by the time they came home, just like me, they were nearing the limit of what they could bear. And this was why they showed no interest in channeling what little energy they had left into pegging up socks or chopping vegetables.

And my husband? Well, by this point in our marriage, Paul was even less interested in domesticity than when we first got together. This was partly my fault. But it wasn't only my fault. Paul, a writer who worked long hours in a wooden cabin at the bottom of the garden, didn't set out to take the path of least resistance on the domestic front. Still, over time he did take it. Staring down middle age, and the pressures of working remotely, he found a way of living with his family all around that allowed him to be at home but not at home and, in this way, to keep his focus on work.

I could have refused to support Paul in this. The reason I didn't urge him to mend his ways domestically, and supported his commitment to work, was that I sympathised with the pressure a writing life brings with it and was loathe to add to it. Besides, it was an arrangement that gave our family a financial stability that my own writing couldn't offer. Certainly there were times when I viewed this arrangement harshly, when the feminist in me viewed it as a cop out. But I also understood how it had come about. This arrangement was confirmed when, in the quiet of my heart following the deaths of Anita and one of my sisters, I decided that my own peace of mind and the well-being of my family was more important than a fair division of household tasks. In the end, my thinking about my home work was that simple.

As for the kids? Was I spoiling them by picking up after them, by refusing to nag them? Perhaps. However, I was confident that they would find out, in their own good time, just how horrid domestic life can be when no-one takes responsibility for it, when hair clogs the shower plug and cheese is left to die at the back of the fridge. One day before too long, they would sleep in dirty bedlinen for however many nights it took them to give up the fantasy of a fairy godmother who swept in and made everything lovely while they were out doing fun things. With any luck, they would overcome their disgust for grotty share houses, not by waving a wand, but by discovering how relatively easy they were to clean up. They would see, as I had, that with a squirty bottle of something, a scratchy cloth and paper towel, that even the most disgusting grot, short of mould in a shower base, can be cleaned away. And in rolling up their sleeves, they would discover the surprising reward of domesticity. Which is that even the plainest of living spaces can be made attractive after a few hours of cleaning it with elbow grease. At which point, the pleasure of coming home to a space that feels ordered, fresh and loved would be theirs.

Even believing this, there were afternoons when I stamped my foot at having to unpack the dishwasher for the umpteenth time as my kids begged off with flimsy excuses of too much schoolwork. Strip away my adult self and I too was still a teenager. Except, I was now middle-aged. And from the middle of my life, a raft of emotions coursed through me to temper my teenage rage. What else did I feel? Thankful for a family life that wasn't punctuated by bursts of temper, as my own upbringing had been. Gratitude to Paul for being willing to be there for the long haul, without expecting me to be the moon that encircled his sun. Pleasure in a daughter who liked walking on bush tracks with head torches in the dark and surfing straight after breakfast, just as much as I did. And a son who, despite hating school, turned to the crossword at the back of the newspaper to read out the clues at breakfast as a matter of course. And a dog who, for all her anxious quirks, glued our family together.

Ideally, the housekeeping role should be shared. Who would dispute this? However, in my household this hasn't been the case. I'm not proud of this. I'm not recommending it. I'm just trying to be honest. And this is why it was me, and not my teenage daughter, who was called Cinderella in our house. I wasn't shoeless. I wasn't sixteen. I didn't wear rags. Yet just like Cinderella, I couldn't just up and leave when I didn't feel like cooking dinner, watering the garden, or straining chicken stock.

Thankfully, there is a flipside, an upside, to household tasks. But there was a hump that I had to clear. There was always an obstacle, mostly in my head, that I had to clear before I reached it. Every Friday afternoon I felt a block that held me back from getting out the vacuum cleaner and duster. It was only once I'd plugged in the vacuum and turned it on that the magic happened. It was as if as I cleaned, I moved through my resistance. And as I did so, I got to know our house all over again. Vacuuming the stairs reacquainted me with them in a way that escaped me when I took them two by two to fetch a jacket for a walk. Far from the burden I feared it would be as a girl, home work grounded me, adding up to a sense of possession or existential ownership that at times I even pitied my family for not sharing.

Each week, I felt a mixture of relief and pride on finishing the housework. This felt well earned. I'd overcome my resistance to cleaning. I'd paid the price that was the cost of living in a cared-for space. I'd sidelined the 'what does it matter if it's clean or not voice' in my head. And after, sitting in the sun on the doorstep, a cup of tea in my hand, I reveled in a job well done. As I returned my cup to the kitchen, taking in the lift and freshness of the rooms I passed through, I gave silent thanks for a home worth loving.

I wasn't a disciplined cleaner. I never washed walls and only occasionally got around to wiping the skirting boards and picture frames. Years would pass by before I forced myself to take down the curtains to be cleaned, and twice a year I happily paid for someone to clean our windows. Yet even my basic weekly clean motivated me to do other homely things, to move furniture around, to peer into the freezer, and to put stray items into a bag I kept for charity. In ways like these, I stayed on top of the running of my home, rather than the other way around.

I felt a similar resistance before doing yoga stretches in the morning. Only with yoga I made nothing of my resistance. I stretched anyway and enjoyed the benefits throughout the day. And it was the same with house-keeping. Rather than waiting until I was in the mood, I got out the vacuum and mop because it was Friday afternoon, confident that my reluctance to clean would dissolve once I did up my apron and filled the sink with soapy water and some drops of lavender oil.

It was a similar story in the bathroom. After brushing my teeth in the morning, I wiped down the basin with a cloth. This was a small thing, so small I hesitate to mention it. And yet it was these small things, done regularly, that had the effect of turning around my domestic feelings from prickly resentment into calm acceptance. Wiping the bathroom basin each morning sent my unconscious the message that staying on top of housework wasn't just possible, it was easy. I didn't have to ask my family to stop splattering the mirror with toothpaste. I could simply do my future self a favour by wiping down the glass and basin in preparation for the rest of the day.

This thinking carried over into other areas of my life. Whenever I went off on holiday, pulling the front door closed and escaping home work for a while, I cleaned up the house first. This made the day before I went away stressful, and I was often late to bed before an early departure. However it was something that I learned to do in order to enjoy coming home. Arriving home, after being away, was always the same. I walked up the path, put my key in the lock and crossed the threshold. For one long second, I looked around our home as a visitor might. The carpets and furniture seemed more colourful than I remembered them. There was a slightly musty, shut-up smell. The pictures on the walls caught the afternoon light in a way that drew my eye to them. Did I, in this second, see my home more truly than I normally did? Then the spell broke, I opened the back door to let in a breeze, and wandered out to see how the garden had fared in my absence. I was home.

One summer, the kids and I went on holiday to my family's beach-house interstate, leaving Paul at home to work. Before our return, I booked a cleaner to come to our house. I rarely gave myself presents but this one I felt I deserved. Brilliant House Cleaning, with five-star reviews topped my internet search. When I explained to the manager, Annette, that I was after a one-off clean before returning from holiday, she laughed. 'I've just booked someone in to clean my own place', she said. 'I've been that busy, run off my feet at work, that I never get around to cleaning my own house.'

Three weeks later, waiting to board the ferry home, I got a text from Paul. 'The cleaners are here!' Then, shortly after boarding, 'The cleaners have gone.' Next day, we arrived home, tired and hungry. I opened the front door gingerly, hopefully. Nothing special met my eye. Everything seemed much as I'd left it. The stairs were clean and the floors looked mopped, but that was it. But something was different. The house smelled lovely, fresher than when we'd left it. Outside the garden had been dowsed with summer rain. I felt a rush of gratitude, both to Annette and to be home.

Under a glass on the kitchen table was an invoice. I stared at the amount. It had taken Annette and her daughter two hours to clean our house from top to bottom, including the basement, amounting to a four-hour fee. I struggled to remember the last time I'd spent four hours cleaning our house, and realised how little I usually got away with.

The next day I rang Brilliant House Cleaning to tell Annette how nice it was to come home to a clean house.

'Don't worry', she chuckled, 'your home wasn't filthy.'

'Really?' I said. 'That's good to hear. In that case, I can't wait to go away again.'

Two middle-aged men on low comfy chairs in the middle of a concert-hall stage wasn't exactly jaw-dropping theatre. Yet 1500 of us were there to hear the cooking writer Yoram Ottolenghi and a local chef discuss everything from cut-throat restaurant politics to the pleasures of home cooking. I'd bought my ticket on a hunch. Ottolenghi, famous for creating recipes with up to twenty ingredients, was in town to promote a cookery book with just five ingredients per recipe. This, I felt, was worth the price of a seat.

It was towards the end of the talk that things got interesting. 'When friends come to your place to eat', Ottolenghi said, 'they don't come to be surprised by a new dish. They come because they like you and enjoyed what they ate the last time they came over. They don't come to be impressed by an exotic dish you've never cooked before. They come to chat and share food around the table. They come because they like you.'

I sat up in my seat. I'd left my own kitchen table halfway through dinner, not to hear commercial restaurant gossip, but to think through my own thorny relationship to cooking. I'd come to hear how I might make preparing food – especially for friends – genuinely expressive. In principle, I liked having friends for dinner. But though I cooked quite well, in the hours before guests arrived it unfailingly felt like an effort I'd rather not make.

I had some friends who genuinely loved spending time in the kitchen. A few were trained chefs. Others had immersed themselves in the world of food from a young age. All of them enjoyed cooking for an audience, rarely consulted recipes and never fussed when friends came for a meal. I also had friends who avoided cooking altogether by delegating it to a more able partner, or by eating out whenever possible. One overworked executive I knew chose to microwave herself a frozen meal most nights. Others fell back on a handful of dishes with a minimum of ingredients and time in the kitchen. They ate to live, rather than the other way around. Depending on my mood, I was all these friends. But because I cared about what I ate, and refused to buy frozen meals, easy escapes weren't available to me.

Up on the stage, Ottolenghi was suggesting a solution to my dilemma so obvious that I'd been blind to it. A student of politics who never trained as a chef, Ottolenghi learned to cook as a hungry university student when he found himself, far from home, missing his mother's Middle Eastern and his father's Italian cooking. Like the audience in front of him, he learned to cook out of necessity, by trial and error.

'If you're a home cook, be a good home a cook', said Ottolenghi, turning to face the audience. 'Don't try to be a chef. Also, please don't be put off by television cooking shows. Home cooking is at an all-time low, while ratings for cooking shows are at an all-time high. Forget about technique. Just cook the dishes that you like and your family and friends will like them too. You really don't have to know how to cook everything. When friends come over, the last thing they want is a stressed-out host who can't relax until the dessert is served. And there's really no rule about serving consecutive courses. A home kitchen isn't a restaurant kitchen, with a sous chef on hand to time courses. Please don't add to the pressure by trying to keep dishes hot. You can't. They'll just dry out. It's much better to put everything in the middle of the table, on nice platters and bowls, and then sit back and enjoy.'

I felt a weight lift off my shoulders. In order to feel comfortable in the kitchen, I didn't have to perfect my knife skills. I didn't have to fork out for an expensive cooking course at an inconvenient time and place. This cooking writer wasn't suggesting complicated menu plans, or pricy ingredients (although he was keen on a rose Harissa paste that was only available on his on-line shop).

'If you're a home cook', Ottolenghi said, warming to his theme, 'and let's be honest, most of us are home cooks, you only need to know how to cook twelve dishes. Good cooking is all about practice, and being in the kitchen is a matter of confidence. So it makes sense to focus on a fixed number of dishes, a repertoire if you like, which you can expand on and adapt, and is always in your head to fall back on. You know what I mean. One great soup. One risotto or rice dish. A vegetable dish that doesn't have vegetarian stamped all over it. An amazing dessert. A meal-in-itself salad. A roast that can be barbecued in summer and warm the house in winter. A cake that makes itself. This really is all you have to do. If you can get these core dishes right, that's totally enough. You can tweak them as much as you like. I know I do. But until you get the timing right – and cooking is all about timing – you'll never feel competent in the kitchen. And timing comes down to practice, doing the same thing over and over until your brain knows what to do without you telling it. At the end of the day, cooking well is about having the confidence to put food together easily in your kitchen, before sitting back and sharing it.'

There was a hush in the auditorium. The man on my left dropped his phone into his lap. Clearly what Ottolenghi was proposing was not just a revelation to me.

Next morning I sat down after breakfast with a pad. It felt ridiculously simple to write down my twelve core dishes. I didn't dither. I wasn't beset by the kind of indecision that usually preys on me when I plan meals. I just noted down the dishes that work best in my kitchen and worked back from that. Once it was done, I looked down at the list. I'd cheated a little by extending the categories. Still, I had my list. At the top was roast chicken, a staple with my family. Next came chicken soup, an old friend. Then a ragu sauce, served with pasta or rice. Eggs came next, baked in the oven with sumac and tomato, or perhaps folded into an omelette. In fifth place was bolognese sauce, another old friend, made with red wine and chicken stock, which I served with pasta, layered into lasagne, or tucked under mashed potato in a cottage pie or spiced into chili con carne. Next came fish, crumbed with polenta and cooked in a pan, or mashed up with potato, parmesan, parsley and spring onion into fish cakes. A mild curry was number seven. My number eight was risotto, thickened with butter and chicken stock and sauteed vegetables. For birthdays and special occasions, I plumped for carrot cake, made with oil, eggs, walnuts and a lemon icing. My easy dessert was fruit crumble with oats and nutmeg. At number eleven was sourdough bread, made from my trusty starter that lives in the fridge. And last of all, an occasional Sunday flourish, was homemade pizza.

Putting down my mug I looked at my list. It was a relief to admit that I didn't want to be, nor needed to become, a great cook. I could grow in confidence without having to master scores of recipes. I could be a minimalist cook and feel no shame in that. Just as I didn't aspire to be a great artist, yet loved to draw, I didn't have to be a great cook. Still it was in my power to be a good enough home cook. And I really wanted to be that.

Something changed, inside my head, once I netted my twelve dishes. Having this list had the effect of making the dishes on it seem more interesting, more 'mine'. I felt less daunted, less threatened by the whole business of cooking. I flicked through cookbooks at the kitchen table, using the index at the back rather than being transfixed by the list of contents at the front. I planned meals ahead, noting ingredients on a pad which I kept in my bag for when I went shopping. Without putting anything into words, I felt a lifting of pressure. By simplifying what I cooked, I appreciated my efforts more. I was cooking to satisfy myself first, rather than to please family and friends. And the best part was that, as if by magic, my family started getting up and doing the dishes at the end of a meal as a matter of course.

11. precious things

My mother had left her house in order. Thanks to my younger sister's help, she hadn't left her house full of stuff. The cupboards that weren't already empty, contained only things she cared about and wanted to pass on to the right person. She couldn't be around forever, she'd lived a good long life. But she could leave my sisters and me her treasures. In this exchange, we'd be reminded of a life well lived and be inspired to do the same.

A month after Mum moved out of the house she lived in for 25 years, and into a nursing home, my family and I flew to Adelaide. My sisters were there too, after arranging to meet to divide up what was left of Mum's belongings.

It was the morning after we arrived. Paul and I were chatting in Mum's courtyard when he received an important call. I got up from the stone wall I'd been sitting on and wandered off to look at the garden. A plane flew overhead, low enough to read 'Virgin' in red letters across its belly. Just off the courtyard was a garden shed. I slid open the door bolt and peered in to find it tidy and spiderweb free. Hardly a garden shed at all. Tools were lined up on fixings against the wall, ready for their next outing. A single wooden cupboard hung on one wall. Inside it, with labels facing out, were insect spray, fertilizer pellets, lime, string and clean gloves. Mum, who'd gardened as intuitively as she'd mothered, had left everything in order here too.

'You know', I said to Paul, after his call had finished, 'what I'd really like to take is this garden. Especially that flower bed over there, with climbing jasmine behind.'

Paul laughed. 'Yes, it is lovely. But then so is our garden at home.'

'Sure', I said, noticing the irrigation drips snaking over the lip of two half wooden barrels, an olive tree in each. 'Except that I'll never garden as well as Mum has done.'

I opened the glass door into the living room, with its plumped up double sofa and armchairs in matching chintz. Built-in bookcases sat either side of a gas fire with a mantlepiece and large mirror above.

'What about this grandfather clock?' I called to Paul as I passed from the living room into the hall. I stared at the clock. It seemed less forbidding now that I was eye height with its face, rather than, as a child, having it frown down from above. 'Is this something that could work for us?'

'Of course, although one of your sisters might want that. Hey', said Paul, pointing to a table in the living room on which a tray of glass decanters; whisky, brandy and gin had sat for as long as I could remember. 'This is a lovely half table.'

Opposite the grandfather clock stood a tall cupboard which opened into a desk. Curiously I opened the doors beneath the drawer with a tiny key. Inside was folded wrapping paper, notepaper, stamps and envelopes, all neatly ordered. In one corner of the cupboard sat a stack of small diaries, a tiny pencil tucked into the spine of each. I leafed through one and then another, the pages squeezed tight with sensible middle-class living – sports events, charity meetings and health appointments. Closing the cupboard, I turned to kneel in front of the chest of drawers opposite. Small tools were in the top drawer, keys in another, board games in the middle drawer, table cloths, bridge pads and playing cards in the bottom drawer. Just as in the linen cupboard of my childhood, everything in Mum's house had its place.

The following afternoon, after a morning spent dividing Mum's things between my sisters and me, Paul and I visited Mum in her nursing home. The wind was shaking a cedar tree outside her third-floor window in an irritated way. Her favourite watercolour, of a dry creek bed and gum trees, hung on the wall above the winged chair she always sat in. Two mahogany chairs, its seats covered in tapestries her own mother had stitched, sat either side of the table on which, for years, she'd played her weekly game of bridge.

It was comforting to see Mum surrounded by her familiar things. The room felt calm and well thought out. Yet she seemed agitated, like she needed to be soothed. She stared into my eyes, clasping my warm hands into her cool ones. 'So', she asked, 'did you get some of the things you wanted?'

'Yes, I got lots of lovely things.' I listed them, noting surprise in her eyes when I mentioned the grandfather clock and the dining table. Then her face softened, her grip loosened and she sank back in her chair. Another load was off her mind, one more transfer of love. This, she told me without words, was all that she could give me now – a dining table, a clock, paintings, cutlery and a rug. Except that we both knew how big these things really were. Their market value was irrelevant, she had loved them for their beauty, and they had buoyed her over the years. Now that her life was nearing its end, she hoped that they would give my sisters and me pleasure for the rest of ours. She took great comfort in knowing that her precious things would come to rest in her daughters' homes across Australia.

Next morning, I returned to Mum's house to put the things I'd chosen into a pile for a courier to collect. Overnight something had happened to them. The side table, shorn of its drinks tray, looked forlorn. Pulled out from the wall, the grandfather clock resumed its familiar frown. The rolled-up carpet looked like a garage-sale offering. What had I done? Had I cut the shimmering threads that held these things in place for so long? Now they were just a stack of objects with my name on a white office sticker on each.

Feeling confused and tearful, I let myself into the garden. I was thrilled to receive these family things. But also appalled. Was this really all that was left of my childhood, side tables, napkin rings and mustard dishes? And had I really put my hand up for the dining table that symbolised everything I was trying to escape from when I left Australia in my early twenties? Needing to sit, I found the low stone wall warm from the sun, the same wall I'd sat on the morning before. So much had happened since then.

A plane flew low overhead. In two weeks' time, when a courier delivered the things stacked up inside to my home in Hobart, how would I feel? Would I be strong enough to stop them from turning into clutter, into stuff? Would I be brave enough, big enough, to give them a place in my heart? And would my own family, who hadn't grown up around these things, get them and love them?

Standing in Mum's garden, it felt all wrong that her furniture and paintings had been plucked from the rooms where they were dusted and polished for decades. I glanced into the living room. Most of the furniture had been cleared away and, with only half the books in the bookcase remaining, those that were left had flopped on their sides. Near the window, the carpet was bleached yellow by the sun, except for two green squares over which two chairs had sat sentinel until the day before. All that remained, at the corner of each green square, was a small indent where the chair legs had dug into the pile.

Two weeks later, back home, at the end of a late-night phone call with Mum, I reminded her of how when I was a girl, we used to quibble over whether she should take a present to the friend she was planning to visit. She liked to make a posy from the garden or, if she was rushing, tie a ribbon round a packet of shortbread. In her mind this was just good manners. For me, it was unnecessary, embarrassing even. Softened by this memory, Mum asked me a question.

'You know', she said, 'sometimes, when I look back over my life, I wonder whether I've ever been really good at anything.'

'Do you?' I replied in a heartbeat. 'That's easy. You're really good at looking after people and organising things. And', I added, 'at gardens.'

She sounded satisfied with my answer and our conversation drifted on to other things. Then, just as I was about to say goodbye, Mum asked the question that started me off on this journey to understand my relationship to home.

'Do you think', she asked, 'that I've wasted my life?' For a second, I had no big thoughts. Glancing at my watch, I saw that it was 11pm and decided I'd called her too late. Was she drowsy? Could she really mean what she'd just asked me?

'Course not', I said, brushing off her question. 'Of course you haven't.' I rattled off a list of her achievements.

After ending our call, I sat on the back doorstep and gazed out to the garden lit up by moonlight. Mum had spent a large part of her life holding her family and home together. Now that she was climbing into her eighties, she was doubting her choices. Propped up in bed, a cup of tea gone cold by her side, she was looking within and asking if she'd come up short. Or was she just feeling tired and lonely on a Sunday night?

If I was convinced of anything as a girl, it was that I wouldn't share my mother's fate. I would never busy myself with school fetes, sports events and hospital visits. But as it turned out, I wound up doing many of these things. Did that mean I would one day ask one of my own kids what Mum had just asked me? If so, how would they answer? I felt sure they'd have something nice to say. Still, the question of what they might really think haunted me. Would they sit by their back door, as I was now, wondering whether their mother had wasted her one and only precious life? It was the hardest question of my life and I still couldn't answer it.

Staring up at the stars, it struck me how skewed my early memories of my mother were. Fixed on her moments of temper, her fiery meltdowns, I recalled her slamming cupboard doors in the kitchen, but not what she bought me for my birthday. I recalled her forcing me to clean up my bedroom, but not her showers of affection. Moments when I bumped into her defences, her hedgehog bristles, kept bubbling up, but not her warm hugs. And yet now that she was nearing the end of her life, memories of her love came streaming back. They were there all along, I just hadn't joined up the dots.

Only looking back, as a mother and wife myself, did those dots become one clear line. Spelling out her love for me and my sisters had never been Mum's thing. It was demonstrating it that was native to her. When I was sick as a child, she brought me my favourite food on a tray. After my father died, we took countless beach walks together. During my early years in London, she penned a constant stream of letters. More recently, she'd be there at the end of the phone, sensing when I might need her.

'Coming?' called Paul from the bedroom.

'Coming', I replied, unmoving.

Growing up, I'd taken it for granted that Mum found family life stressful. This wasn't my imagination. Bringing up four girls in a big house had been a constant source of tension for her. However what I'd failed to see was that this tension was the price she was willing to pay for the sake of something greater, family love. I'd overlooked the richness she found in family life, and the pleasure she took from an attractive home. I'd missed the joy that she got from working in the garden, her delight in the small successes of my sisters and I, the depth of her marriage, her close friends. How had all this richness escaped me? Was it because it was so ordinary, so seemingly normal?

When I was the age my own kids were now, I'd discounted my mother's love for my sisters and me. It was fussing. It was nagging. What I didn't understand back then, what I couldn't fathom in my pig-headed adolescence, was the extent to which loving someone *is* to look after them. Aged sixteen, I refused to accept, it was incomprehensible to me, that loving someone is inseparable from caring for them practically, emotionally and soulfully.

Sitting up late on my back doorstep, I'd looked after myself without my mother's help for decades. Even so, there were still times when I struggled to do this. What did it mean, to look after myself anyway? Even the grammar seemed clumsy. Could this explain why I found the process of looking after my family and home easier than looking after myself? Was this why I found it easier to anticipate my family's needs and desires than to look out for my own? I knew it shouldn't be this way. But it was. Looking after myself didn't come any more naturally to me now, sitting in the moonlight when I should have been asleep, than when I was a girl. Would I always feel challenged by this? Would I always have to crane to hear what I wanted above the din of family life? Would ringfencing time and energy, so that I had some left to satisfy my desires, always feel like an indulgence? Would I always struggle to experience myself in the round, rather than just paddling to keep up? Could I trust myself to leave the housekeeping aside, to take time off from tasks that I didn't ultimately care about, to make room for activities that I cared about? Could I leave off worrying about whether things were worthwhile or not and just do them because I loved doing them?

⅓

A few nights after the call with my mother, Paul and I were lying in bed. The clock on the bedside table told me it was after midnight.

'I read that Marie Kondo book, you know, the one about tidying up, that you left on the stairs', Paul said into the darkness.

'Oh yeah, and what did you think?'

'I found it quite seductive. She seems remarkably unburdened by what other people might think of her ideas.'

'Mmm, I think that's what I find refreshing. Even her tone is innocent.'

I fell quiet, sensing where this might be going. Over the years we'd lived in our big old house, the lower steps of the stairs had become a hold-all for books and other small items I'd pick up on my way to the bedrooms above. Sundry items, like toothpaste and soap, awaited collection on one step. A basket of clean folded laundry might rest on another. Library books had a step all of their own, the easier to grab when it was time to return them. Emma's phone and wallet, which otherwise went walkabout, sat on another.

I knew Paul disliked the stairs being used in this way. I knew that whatever was on the stairs caught his eye when he opened the front door, and that this bothered him. 'Why', I imagined him asking, 'does Helen flag her housekeeping in this way, when she knows I have no objection to it but just don't have time for it myself?' The stuff on the stairs caught my eye too. 'Do my bidding!' the toothpaste called, as I took the stairs two by two on another mission altogether. 'Look at us!' said the pile of folded clothes as I brushed past them. 'We are domestic life', they chorused, 'minus the fairies to whisk us about.'

During the lull in conversation, I considered the wisdom of ending it there. But Paul pushed on. 'You know, reading that Kondo book wound me up quite a bit. I think I share some of her obsessiveness.'

'Do you mean that you'd like our house was tidier?' I asked, wishing we were both sound asleep.

'Yes, I know it annoys you for me to say. But I really do. There's a bit in her book where she talks about other people's mess. She says that, in the end, you can only really clear up your own mess, you can only look after your own space, and that after that you have to hope that the people you live with will get the hint and clear up their mess. Only', he ended punchily, 'they don't.'

Lying in the dark, I told myself not to react. What about your clothes cupboard, I wanted to ask, fuming, which is always as messy as can be? Paul rolled on to his shoulder, facing away. A welcome breeze came through the window.

I was unable to contain myself. 'You know that I work my guts out in this house. And that, if I didn't spend as much time as I do putting things away, it would be much, much messier?' Paul rolled back to face the ceiling. 'And it winds me up when you say that our house is messy when really it isn't.'

'Yes. I'm sorry. But little things get to me in a way that I don't think you realise.'

'And', I said, as if he hadn't spoken, 'I think you know how upset I'll be when our kids aren't here to make a mess anymore, and that I'd rather they were here with their mess than have no mess at all.'

Too incensed to sleep, I took myself off to the sofa bed next door. Staring at the ceiling, it struck me that Paul saw clutter where I saw family life. He wanted to live minimally with clear surfaces and nothing left on the stairs. Just as he longed for symmetry in the garden, he wanted order in our home life. He wanted it to have a predictability that allowed him to focus on his work. He wanted his eye to scan the living room, without it being tripped by a badly-darned rip in the rug. It wasn't just that we had different tastes. We experienced the contours of home life differently. Fond things for me – sports shoes in the hall and a bike leaning against the banister – annoyed him. When he walked into the kitchen late on a Sunday, all he saw was mess, whereas I saw an afternoon of crafting and cooking, a smattering of school homework.

However naïve Marie Kondo sounded, in giving her socks feelings and emptying her handbag each night, she was on to something. She understood how intimate a role my possessions played in my life. She knew that the precious things that Mum had left me were at risk of becoming Paul's clutter. She sensed my guilt for the grandfather clock, parked under the stairs, its pendulum stopped against its penetrating tick-tock. She knew that certain objects had the power to lift me up or pull me down, and that my feelings for them would decide whether I cared for them in years to come, or plotted their demise.

A few days later, I dropped into our local bookshop. It was late on a Sunday just before closing. The bookseller at the till happened to be a friend and a fellow writer. When he asked what I was looking for, I felt embarrassed, knowing how far the title I wanted was from the literary fiction that inspired his own work.

'*The Gentle Art of Swedish Death Cleaning*', he repeated, a querying lilt in his voice. He thought for a moment. 'Oh, *I* know. It's on our landfill table.' With that, he walked me to the front of the shop and plucked a book from a pile on a folding table. I flicked through its pages. In my five-minute glean, Margareta Magnusson convinced me that if I could conquer my resistance to clearing out cupboards, I would have more room in my life for creativity. In losing some of my past, by giving some of it away and discarding the rest, I would clear a path to a better future. Her message was simple. Discovering Magnusson, on the tail of Marie Kondo, was refreshing. Her tone was more down to earth and philosophical than Kondo's. She was witty but also compassionate. 'If you can't deal with your own stuff, while you're still alive,' she wrote drily, 'why should your family be any better at it once you're gone?'

I bought the book and read it in bed that night. On a closer read, Magnusson's main point seemed to relate not so much to death, as to the here and now. Like Marie Kondo, she was alive to the role that my possessions played in my imagination, quite apart from the space they took up at home. In order to expand into the present, she was instructing me to let go of some of my past. If I wasn't to lose myself in lost dreams and what ifs, I would have to farewell quite a lot of stuff. Magnusson wasn't anti-sentimental. She wasn't a silent reaper. She was all for keeping important objects that tied me to myself. But she was against boxing things up in the basement, closing cupboards and hoping for the best.

The following night as the house grew quiet, the lights in my study were still on. A hot night, the window was open to let in a breeze. The dog was asleep in her chair next to me and Paul was working late in the front of the house. I tipped over the twenty-minute timer I keep on my desk for when I need to shut out the world and focus on work, and watched particles of sand drop through the tiny-waisted funnel. Then I knelt on a cushion in front of my study cupboard and started pulling out books and files until the shelves were bare. I'm deciding what I want to keep, I told myself, echoing Kondo, not what I want to throw away.

Two hours later, flipping over the timer one last time, I opened the broom cupboard next to my study cupboard. Even as I opened these doors, I knew that I wasn't going to toss out anything in this closet. But I was curious, and told myself that I'd obey my twenty-minute timer and go to bed once the sand had emptied. Beside the vacuum cleaner, broom, shopping bags, mop and dustpan sat two large sketchpads. Sitting cross-legged on the floor, I flicked through my old drawings. Most of them I'd drawn in my studio flat in London, listening to audiobooks as I recovered from glandular fever. A line drawing of the living room brought my studio flat back to life, from the calico sheet covering the sofa bed, to the Conran lamp on the pine table that overlooked the street. Another was of flowers in a vase, drawn one Easter when I happened to have nowhere to go. I was instantly drawn back to the person I was when I drew these pictures. More than all the notebooks and folders strewn across the floor, these drawings were still alive, beating with a part of myself that I hadn't quite forgotten. As the last of the sand fell through the glass funnel, I slid the sketchpads into the cupboard and returned to the mess of papers on the floor.

Three trips to the rubbish bins later, I went up to bed. Next morning, sunlight peeped through the bedroom curtains. I heard the bin truck stop in front of our house. As the bins were lifted and emptied of notebooks, typescripts, domestic appliance manuals, utility bills and textbooks, I felt lighter. I got out of bed, padded downstairs in my pyjamas and let out the dog. Then I went into my study for the sheer pleasure of opening the cupboard doors and reveling in the appearance of order. Gone were the stacks of notebooks and paperwork, waiting for something, anything, to happen to them. In the next cupboard along, which I didn't open, my sketchbooks sat patiently. Were these, I wondered, part of the future that Magnusson was suggesting I needed to make room for?

CB

Two months after Mum asked me whether she'd wasted her life, she died. Speaking at her funeral, a boiling hot day, I told the people gathered – friends, family, her old gardener and family doctor – that I thought she'd found getting old difficult because her frailty prevented her from showing her love for the people she loved. Looking out from the third floor of her nursing home she had no garden to tend. Years had passed since she'd mulched her garden beds, for fear of tripping over. She couldn't take cuttings from friends' gardens, or make posies for hospital visits. And without these cuttings, these posies, there was no proof of her love.

Mum had gone. Yet her question about the value of how she'd spent her life stayed with me, perhaps because I'd already spent a good part of my own life caring about clean sheets, good food and attractive living spaces. Would I, one day, feel the same regret she had? Would I doubt the value of the time, energy and love that I'd spent caring for family, cooking for friends, growing plants and baking bread? Would I rue not having traveled more, earned more, learned more, networked more? Mum's question stayed with me because it wasn't just her question. It was mine too. Neither of us had spelled it out, but we both knew it was part of a life-long conversation between us about what mattered most. For my part, I felt sure that she didn't regret how she'd spent her days. Had she her life over, I was confident she'd spend them in a similar way. Even so, I felt grateful for her question. Because answering it had prompted me to think long and hard about what home work meant to me.

In the months after Mum's funeral, I enjoyed being on my own at home more than before. Accepting my own mortality by facing hers tilted the axis of my world. I focused on what I wanted most from life, and left off trying to get everything right. I looked after myself, my family and friends in ways that I felt good about, without worrying about what others might think. I didn't feel beholden to anyone else's vision of a good life – whether it was my husband's or Marie Kondo's. If Paul, or Marie Kondo for that matter, wanted to keep my stairs clear, then by all means they could. But for as long as I was the one running the house, I would live in it the way that made me happiest and most at ease.

Mum's death pushed me to the end of the branch I'd been sitting on my whole life. Now there was nothing but air between me and the ground. This felt liberating, but scary too. Because I no longer felt confident there'd be enough time to do everything I hoped to do in life. This wasn't a bucket-list feeling. It felt more global than that. It was as if the only time that I could be completely sure of was the present moment.

12. kitchen reno

'A calm and modest life brings more happiness than
the pursuit of success combined with constant restlessness.'
Albert Einstein

During my early thirties, I was drawn to magazine stories about stylish women with small children and a busy working life. These women, just a few years older than myself, seemed to have figured it all out. Reading about their lives gave me hope. If I went on to have children, I too could expect my life to be messy and busy but basically good. My mornings would be rushed. I'd drink cold tea on the fly and have less time to myself. But I felt confident that my life as a whole would be richer for having a family at the middle of it.

With hindsight, I realise that these stories were written from the outside looking in, by a journalist with her finger on a record button and an afternoon deadline. They weren't written from inside the mind of the woman profiled, who probably forgot what she'd told the journalist by the time the story was published. Just as the editor of the magazine intended, the stylish mayhem of these families was aimed at beguiling women like me. A dog wandered through an open door, lunchboxes lay open on otherwise clear benchtops, morning sun filtered through a sparkling kitchen window. There were no regrets in these photos, no toddler meltdowns, no work deadlines, no smudged mascara, no mortgage stress. There was no to-do list that these women needed to tick off before school pick-up, for fear of all hell breaking loose before nightfall. Everything was captured in this casual moment of insouciance, a freeze frame of a day about to happen. It didn't looked staged to me. It looked just like a life I might want for myself.

In many ways, I have lived that life. For years, I made my kids breakfast in a lovely kitchen as I filled lunchboxes and drank tea on the fly. I have lived the life that I hoped to lead. However it would be dishonest not to admit that at times it seemed that all I was doing was creating a set of demands for myself. I was trying, and often failing, to rise to them. Daydreaming about what family life might be like was easy in my early thirties. Housekeeping for the family that I went on to have, as the years galloped by, was more challenging and time-consuming than I'd ever imagined.

Over the years, housekeeping has required quite a lot of courage from me. This isn't a quality normally associated with home life. Yet it chimes with my experience of it. It takes courage to push aside my noisy ego when I'm not in the mood to cook, and to bring to mind the pleasure and relief that a good meal brings. Hanging out wet bedlinen on a sunny day, or arranging a roof repair on a wet one, these assume that I'm able to overcome my resistance to doing such tasks in the first place. Caring about the hundred and one things that a well-run home assumes takes a surprising amount of strength.

When I was a girl, I had no idea that when I grew up there would be no such thing as later. I had to become an adult myself before it dawned on me that I could be as wild and expansive with my dreams as I liked, but unless I acted on them they'd stay locked inside of me. When it finally sank in that there was no later, I felt excited and nervous. But also oddly relieved. Because it meant that I could stop waiting for the right time to do things, and just get on with them there and then. I started opening mail at the front door rather than leaving it unopened on the hall table. I paired socks at the clothes line rather than tossing them loose into the basket. I sent shorter emails for the pleasure of pressing 'send' sooner. Small actions like these helped me to feel competent, expedient, because I wasn't clogging up my future with things I knew I wouldn't want to do then either. This had an unintended but welcome result. I feared what was around the corner less because, in a way, I was already dealing with it. Most of all, I stopped expecting my family to ease my load and made the domestic sphere more fully my own. And in accepting all this, in recognising that this was my one precious life, I felt a whole lot freer.

If I hadn't had a controlling mother, nagging my family to step up domestically may not have been an issue for me. I could have plastered rosters to the fridge and withheld pocket money when my kids failed to pull their weight. But I've rarely been stern with my kids, nor felt inclined to be. Instead I took inspiration from my godmother, who once told me how, as a girl, she refused to make her bed and tidy her room, even when her mother kept on at her. Rather than get annoyed, her mother had laughed at her daughter's refusal. Don't worry she would call out to Sue, playing in the garden, your time will come! I found this story heartening because it gave me permission to stop nagging my kids. It told me that it wasn't my job to domesticate my family. My job was to get on with my life and to like who I was, safe in the knowledge that one day my kids' turn would come.

og

A few months after my mother's funeral, Alex decamped from his bedroom upstairs to the damp spare room downstairs, as far away from family as possible without actually moving out. For a month his old room remained untouched. A large desk pushed into the bay window was covered with paint tubes, screwdrivers, scissors, sports medals, coins, hand tools, opened letters and certificates. A film of dust covered the lot. A sofa bed flanked the wall opposite the fireplace with cherry-picked bookcases either side.

One weekend I hauled everything Alex had left behind onto the rug and badgered him to sort it out. Once cornered, it took him a few quiet hours to sort his childhood into three messy piles: things to keep; things to give away; and things to throw. Magazines, books and photos were kept. Wooden blocks, Meccano and Lego were packed away in the basement. Paints, glues, tools, brushes, plane kits, model planes filled a box to be given away. Bits of boats and bikes went into a garbage bag. One trip to the recycle shop later and the room was all but empty. It felt like a miracle. The years spent nagging Alex to clean up his room were over.

I didn't want the master bedroom to be a sad room. I didn't want a museum of childhood off our upstairs landing. The room needed new life and I sensed where to take it. A pale painted floor, a subdued yet colourful rug and cream furniture. A work table under the bay window and a cupboard for childhood things that none of us wanted to part with. That was it.

For weeks, I tried to cajole myself into painting the room. I even tried bribing myself. No good. Everything felt more pressing than tipping paint into a tray and dipping a roller into it. Another month passed. Until one night, when Paul went interstate at short notice, I picked up a paint roller and got to work. A few hours later, I laid down the roller. It was after midnight, the house was asleep and the floors I'd once stained chocolate brown were now a creamy white.

There were still the walls, mantlepiece and skirting boards to paint, plus two more floor coats. Before each painting session, I rebelled against putting on my painting clothes. My kids weren't exactly encouraging. 'It's like a milk factory in here', said Alex, smattered with mud after a bike ride. 'A trip to Sweden?' asked Emma, home from school. On Paul's return, he glanced around the room and said with a quick smile, 'It looks fine.' Personally, I loved the changes. I loved that after all this time I'd decorated a room the way I liked it, with no aim to please anyone but myself. Late at night, I'd stretch out on the sofa bed with a book and a hot drink, my own little ship in the night.

When first renovating the house, I'd kept the color scheme simple, painting the walls off white and adding deeper tones to just a few rooms. The renovation was so daunting that it seemed the sanest approach. The weekend after I finished decorating, a friend from Melbourne visited to celebrate the end of our renovation. A week later, a parcel arrived by post. It was a thank you from my friend, a coffee table book of English interiors. Many a night after that I stayed up late, admiring the cool elegance of the rooms in the book. The colours of the rooms drew me in. I loved even their names: dove grey; gunshot; moonshine; and blood orange. It was one thing admiring the carefully styled rooms painted blue wren and moss green. But could my fancies be trusted? Was I being taken in by clever photography and artful styling? Eventually, unable to answer this question, I slipped the book between cookery books in the pantry. Now and then I took it down for a quick flick through when I should have been cooking. But I gave up the idea of transforming the house by painting each room a different colour.

A few months after I repainted Alex's old room, I picked up a design magazine in the library and instantly fell in love with the kitchen on its cover. The whites, greys and unpainted wood chimed so completely that I decided to use it as a model to turn our kitchen around in the two weeks of school holidays remaining. Five years had passed since Paul and I made up our renovation as we went along. This time round, I would flesh out my ideas with a professional first. A local architect agreed to a one-off consult. He arrived on time, wearing a black t-shirt and jeans, a notebook hugged to his chest. For the next hour, we chatted through various options, before he gave me his opinion. 'What I find, as an architect, is that the kitchen tends to be the most expensive room in the house.'

'Yes', I agreed, sensing his drift.

'Given that you're drawn to a Nordic look', he said, 'I'd advise ripping out your kitchen and starting again from scratch.' Disheartened by the ball-park figure he gave, and at the waste of ripping out a perfectly good kitchen bench, I gave up my project even before I thanked him and showed him out.

That night, I picked up the design magazine sitting on the kitchen table. Even as I told myself to put it down, I opened it up and placed the spread of photos I liked under the bright light of the hob. Then I looked at each photo long and hard, now and then glancing up at the cooking oil smattered on the wall above. Renovating, I told myself, was a first-world problem. Caring about the look of my kitchen was vanity. But still I wanted it. Letting out a sigh, I leaned against the hob and let my imagination roam. I saw a tall kitchen table in the middle of the room, the same height as the waist-high bench. An arc floor lamp reached from the window to the middle of the table. And a high, buff-coloured bench. In a rush of confidence, I vowed that, in the ten days before school went back, I'd renovate the kitchen myself.

Selecting a colour for the kitchen cupboards was only slightly harder than the dizzying choice of colours for the bench. But not as hard as putting on my painting clothes, rolled up at the back of my wardrobe. I liked so many of the colours in the coffee table book that choosing just one felt impossible. Did I really love the stone blue and moss green in the photos I was staring at? Or did I envy the lives of the people who lived in rooms painted these colours?

Emma got busy for a fee in the basement, making a waist-high kitchen table from new floorboards and old round fence posts that she later painted white. Not exactly Nordic, but inexpensive, striking and strong. When I took the interiors book to the paint shop, the assistant was unable to match the blue-grey shade I wanted on the colour chart. So I chose a duck-egg blue which was on the chart, but when I came home with it in sample pots, it lacked the depth and subtlety of the shade in the interiors book, even after three days of living with it on two cupboard doors and willing myself to like it.

I was walking the dog along the beach when I realised that, much as I wanted to be someone who experimented with colour in the kitchen, I wasn't that person. I wanted light and space in the room that I spent most time in. I didn't want my eye to be drawn to a bold colour on the cheap cupboard doors I'd opted for when our renovating budget had dried up. My mind was made up and I'd been trying to override it. And so, after stamping the sand off my shoes and coaxing the dog into the car, I drove to the paint shop and returned home with low-sheen Organic Cotton for the cupboard doors and a beige classic Hog's Bristle for the walls.

The next three days I spent painting. Listening to my kids' song lists and various podcasts, I repainted the cupboards and then the walls. I also listened to a torrent of news, stunned at how many world events could unfold in the time that it took to paint one kitchen and pantry. As I waited for the paint to dry, I searched online for a floor lamp, in turn lost in admiration for Scandinavian design, and disgusted that so many copies of the lamp I liked should be sitting in warehouses around the world. And I chased local joiners, none of whom sounded keen to make a single kitchen cupboard to put in a fireplace arch when plenty of clients wanted to pull out their kitchen and start over.

A week later, with the kitchen bench installed, I took up the dust sheets, scraped paint blobs off the floorboards and put the paint pots away. I looked around. It wasn't my fantasy kitchen. It could never be mistaken for the cover of a design magazine. And my lower back ached from skipping yoga and lugging paint pots and ladders around. Still, I was thrilled to have brought about a change I'd been longing for.

That night after dinner, Paul and I stood silently in the kitchen, amazed at the transformation of a space that had staged so much family life. Birthdays and school homework and board games would now take place at this higher table under a brighter light. And I was looking forward to that.

The metre-high table dominated the room. At night, the arc floor lamp pooled light from above as we ate dinner. The dark wood table top was shiny with a varnish that I hadn't wanted, but turned out to be the practical choice. I loved that table. Not just because Emma made it. But because having a high table in the middle of the kitchen changed the space dramatically. It signaled to me that I didn't know what was coming next. And that just when I thought I knew what I wanted, something else, even better, came along to surprise me.

☙

The last time Paul had a big birthday we seated forty people along trestle tables on our verandah in Melbourne, with hired glasses and chaos in the kitchen. After serving the starter, a friend came into the kitchen as I

135

washed grit from leeks under the tap. 'Haven't you washed those already?' she asked, surprised.

'No', I said, embarrassed.

She laughed. 'My mother's a caterer. Which means that whenever she entertains, everything is prepped and planned hours ahead.'

'Well', I said, waving a wet hand at the noisy guests out the window, 'if I'd planned this ahead of time, I'd never have invited this many people!'

The next time Paul had a big birthday, the guest list was shorter. But I still spent the morning before in a mild panic. Had I cooked enough food? Would I have to pretend to be relaxed when guests arrived? Could we really pull this off? As chance would have it, our dishwasher had broken weeks before and I was waiting for a pump to arrive at the appliance repair shop. When I called the shop to enquire after the pump, the woman on the phone sounded surprised to hear tears creep into my voice.

I needed a walk to clear my head, to see sky above and not the kitchen around me. Snapping on the dog's lead, I drove to a bush track near our house. Under the cover of gum trees, I started to cry. I cried for the years that had passed with nothing yet everything to show for them. I cried for the friends travelling from interstate as a surprise for Paul, who was working as hard as ever, even on his birthday. I cried for my marriage, which at times felt out of my hands, yet I knew was cradled within them. I cried for a family life which at times felt so consuming, demanding and rewarding I could barely hear myself think. And I cried for my kids who I was in the slow process of letting go, of letting down, so they could make lives of their own.

As suddenly as they'd started, like a sun shower, my tears stopped. I looked up at the trees, thanked them for their shelter and stepped into the sun feeling lighter.

Two hours before the guests were due, Emma stopped me in the kitchen. 'Will you be glad when this dinner is over?' she asked, upside down wine glasses in each hand. 'Gosh', I said, putting down a tray of cutlery, 'that's a good question. Well yes, I'll be glad not to be in a panic. But no. I really want to have this dinner. I want to see how it goes and would hate it to be over already.'

As guests streamed through the front door, my excitement mounted. Standing at the kitchen window, I counted heads in the courtyard below; seventeen, eighteen, nineteen, twenty, I counted, including Paul and me. There was another knock at the door. I opened it.

'That means', I said, 'that you are twenty-one and twenty-two!' And we laughed as I ushered them through the hall. Emma took the change in her stride, shuffling place settings around and fetching stools from upstairs. There was another knock at the door.

'Have you forgotten how to count?' asked Emma, rolling her eyes at a mother who didn't know how many people she'd invited for dinner.

Getting twenty-four adults around one long table felt like herding cats. Some chatted in the hall, others gossiped in the kitchen, a few lingered in the courtyard. Two wandered off to explore the garden. None of them wanted to be treated like wedding guests. 'But what about the asparagus?' I asked no-one in particular, pushing through a clutch of people to rescue a steaming pot from the hob.

Then something happened. Two guests decided that they'd rather help out my kids in the kitchen than sit on stools squashed into corners of the table. With this, the four of them took over serving the meal. 'Go away', said Alex, pushing me out of the kitchen, 'we don't need you here.' Leaving them to it, I found my seat at the table. Emma, flushed in shorts and t-shirt, flew in and out of the room, plates piled high. Alex took over the sink, as if it were the galley of the ship that he was on leave from working on as a deckhand. Twice more I entered the kitchen to help serve, and twice more I was sent back to the table.

Towards the end of dinner, a woman I didn't know well tapped me on the shoulder as I removed her plate. 'Your husband is very lucky to have you do all this for him', she said impishly, sipping wine and waving her hand at the rowdy table. As I stacked plates in the kitchen, I thought about this woman's comment. I knew I hadn't cooked for twenty-four people just to please Paul. I'd thrown the dinner as a gift to everyone who'd come. It was for Paul, yes. But it was for our friends just as much. It was to thank them for being in our life and to let them know they were worth cooking for. The woman was right. Paul was lucky. Even so, I didn't feel compromised by throwing a dinner for him. I felt glad to do it.

Paul talked to the people either side of him as if there were no tomorrow, declaring, at the end of the evening, that it had been his best birthday yet. No singing, no speeches, just friendship lighting up the room. I too lost myself in conversation, forgetting the time and that I was meant to be hosting. When I entered the kitchen after dessert, Alex was confident from my laugh that I'd been drinking, which I rarely do. 'Perhaps', I said. 'Though maybe I'm just happy.'

Ↄ

When Wendy Berry applied for a position as Royal Housekeeper, at Prince Charles's Highgrove Estate, the job description was brief. It was 'to streamline and ensure the smooth-running of the household.' When I read this line in Berry's tell-all memoir, standing up in the library, my first thought was, isn't this what it means to look after any home – to streamline and maintain its smooth running? To care about it in a way that leads you to take pride in details that you might otherwise not? To throw a dinner party knowing that you have no control over what guests take away with them once they get up from the table?

A few days after the party, I took down a dictionary to look up the word 'pride'. The first meaning it gave was 'to have an unduly high regard for oneself.' No, I thought, that wasn't what I felt as I put the vacuum cleaner away for the week. The second definition also missed the mark: 'proper pride; a sense of what befits one's position, preventing one of doing unworthy thing'. This wasn't what I felt either, I thought, returning the book to the shelf. I didn't feel too good to clean. I was perfectly willing to clean up after myself. It was another kind of pride that got me over the hump that

I had to clear whenever I didn't feel like housekeeping. This kind of pride encouraged me to live up to my own standards, rather than listening to my resistance to household tasks whisper to me that I had better things to do. This pride told me that it was worth sprinkling peppercorns into chicken stock and stripping linen from a bed, even when I was in a rush. This pride, this quiet dignity, stopped me from letting myself down. And it was in living up to my own standards, in all these ways, that I became worthy of my own love, which is perhaps the most precious love of all.

Once upon a time, I vacuumed and mopped because I had to. I house-kept because my flatmates expected it, because I'd internalised my mother's high standards and because I didn't want to live in a pigsty. Housekeeping felt like a neverending task that only took from me. However, over the years, housekeeping, family love and the domestic arts had joined up to become something else, something greater. It had become home work, a way of life that gave me a deep satisfaction distinct from achievement, a peace of mind and inner richness that I still struggle to find words for.

What I do know, and do have words for, is just how much love and effort it requires to keep up a warm and attractive home, especially with a family at the middle of it. This labour of love keeps me fit and makes me feel, in some elemental way, that my life is bound up with the nature of things. Far from a bar to worldly success, home work now feels like a preliminary for it.

So much to do with housekeeping involves keeping bacteria at bay, crumbs off the floor, allergies down and the fence posts standing. This is why home work, as a whole, is so important. Because it flags to everyone who comes into your home the more there is to life once the necessities have been satisfied. Tiny victories, like flowers in the bathroom and home-made biscuits in a tin, don't last. They serve as small triumphs over our ego and our infernal busyness.

Inviting friends for dinner, planting seedlings and drawing a birthday card, being creative at home, can be oddly demanding, at times more so than the household tasks and work deadlines that can't be avoided. I put up obstacles to my creativity, even though the effects of it are what make me feel at home. Flowers in the kitchen are a sign to my family that we're worth picking flowers for. I'm pretty sure that no-one in my family views them in this light, but it's how I feel when I pick them and put them in a jug.

The linen cupboard that I now have is nothing like the one I had in my childhood home. It's smaller, less organised and would never fit a five-year old in it. Still, the feel of that original linen cupboard – its sense of safety, comfort and taken for grantedness – was in my mind when we renovated our current home. This was the feeling of homeyness that I was seeking as I painted and stitched. Even with thick curtains, our house can be freezing in winter. But hopefully, it's also welcoming and giving.

These days, so that I have time to play the piano and draw, I have what I call my housekeeping hour. Instead of spreading household tasks across a day – even while sitting in front of a computer, tasks and errands flit through my mind – I give over an hour a day to them. Rather than feeling pulled this way and that by a stream of tasks, I'll do as many as I can inside my housekeeping hour, usually early evening. I don't always succeed. Sometimes I skip the hour altogether. Or I'll split it in two, with half first thing in the morning and the other half before dinner. On the weekend, if the garden or pantry gets the better of me, it might spill into the next hour. It's a kind of discipline to take my apron off when the hour is up. But when I do succeed, setting the kitchen timer and making a game of it, I find I can rake leaves, cook rice, hang laundry, pay bills, change bedlinen, water herbs and repair clothing, and finish the hour feeling better about life than had I not done these things.

I've developed some rules to keep my housekeeping hour on track. I keep a mental list of what needs doing. So my energy doesn't flag, I might make a cup of tea and a snack before I start. I try to put one thing on my list that I don't want to do – often an admin task or a repair – knowing how quickly these can build up and fester. I put my phone on the stairs during this hour, so as not to lose precious time down rabbit burrows. And on Sundays, I might skip the hour altogether.

When I was a teenager, I had no idea that the feeling I sometimes had, of feeling unworthy of love, would later be dissolved by learning to look after myself and my home, by home work. How could I have known that the shame I sometimes felt, back then, of feeling unworthy of the gift of life, would be turned around by the experience of running a home? This sounds sweepingly simple, and clearly as a transformation it hasn't been that. Making the most of my home and family has been far more demanding than my fantasies about family life as a young woman ever were. Still, I now feel connected to the circle of life in a way that I didn't when I was a girl.

The discomfort I felt as a teenager, at being looked after by my mother, has been flipped. In the place of discomfort, lies a confidence in my ability to look after myself. Making the bed, wiping down the kitchen bench and dreaming up something to cook for dinner tell me that I'm up to everything else I have to do that day. Far from being lowly and demeaning, my youthful fear, keeping on top of home life now feels like proof of my competence. Entering the kitchen early each morning, raising the blinds and filling the kettle, I sometimes feel that thanks to my commitment to it, I deserve my lovely home.

What I failed to realise, when I was drawn to magazine stories profiling women with small children and a stylish home life, was the emotional cost of all that love and responsibility. It was only once I encountered the double whammy of motherhood and housekeeping myself, that I realised my mother's temper had been a reaction to stress. It was only when I found myself living under similar pressures myself that I came to sympathise with her flare ups. My response to this pressure was different to hers – my response was to do yoga and not to shout. Still, I did feel this pressure.

Like my mother before me, I've been the one who held things together at home. This role wasn't forced on me. It could have been shared with my husband. But in my case it wasn't. I knew that my days of family housekeeping wouldn't last forever, but at this point it was my job. I picked up groceries on the way home. I folded bedlinen straight off the line, I whisked it off if it looked like rain. I bought bags of compost from road-side stalls. I called the handyman when the dog found a broken paling in the fence. I gave thought to birthdays weeks ahead. At night, I turned off lights and pulled blinds as I passed empty rooms. If tasks like these don't add up to a worthwhile part-time job, I don't know what does.

13. washing up

The first sign that something was seriously amiss in my marriage came a year and a half into the pandemic when Paul stopped doing the washing up after dinner. Without my noticing, from one night to the next, his concession to the evening meal slipped. Normally he hopped up when dinner was over to get the washing up out of the way so that we could start playing the game we usually played after dinner sooner. First, he put any leftovers into a container for someone's lunch the next day – huffing and puffing if he couldn't find the right lid in the pantry. Then he mock scolded the dog who has a disgusting habit of licking dirty dishes as they're stacked in the dishwasher. Then he wiped down the table with the kitchen sponge, before buffing it with a tea-towel. Finally it was time for a game.

Life during the pandemic felt so consuming that I didn't notice Paul had stopped washing up until after he had. Still, the strain in our relationship had been obvious for a while. Paul regularly complained that there wasn't enough food in the pot at dinner, always a bad sign. And he took to having drinks with friends who, he explained, were more fun than me.

Initially I blamed our troubles on Covid. But Paul disagreed. He felt our growing-apartness was the result of life pulling us in different directions. The first time he told me that he wanted to end things between us, he was holding a steaming pot of coffee at the back door. But because he said it in a moment of temper, I decided not to believe him. I put his outburst down to his worry about work and to my coming between him, his writing routine and his morning coffee. Choosing to end our conversation, I walked into the kitchen, snapped on the light above the hob, got out a tub of Gumption and a scourer, and started scrubbing. I knew that cleaning the hob after marital strife was a cliché. I knew that scrubbing around the rings was my attempt to block out Paul's words. But I also knew cleaning the hob calmed me and that whatever did or didn't happen in my marriage, I'd be cleaning the hob for years to come. This thought comforted me. Paul may force me to lose my foothold and, with it, the platform that marriage had for so long provided me. Still, in that moment my sanity was guaranteed by a tub of Gumption, a scourer and my rhythmic scrubbing of the hob.

After Paul's words by the back door, he and I went about our parallel lives. He apologised for his fiery words and I agreed to see a psychologist with him to try to sort things out. But just three weeks into these sessions, Paul told me, quietly and undramatically, over lunch in our favourite café, that he didn't want to be married to me anymore. His feelings for me, he explained, felt closer to that of a relative – a cousin perhaps – than a husband. He'd felt this for a while. After thirty years together, he felt that it was time for him to lead a different kind of life and to be around people who understood him better. Besides, he ended, he'd long wanted to live independently and to spend more time in Europe.

Even in my confusion, it was clear from Paul's calm manner that his mind was made up. His tone was as sorry as it was gentle. Our relationship, he said, at least the married part, was over.

For the next six weeks, Paul went on living in our house. Outwardly, life continued as before, even though inwardly everything had changed. If anything, the atmosphere between Paul and me was better for being less strained. It was as if his honesty, his determination to push through, had cleared a space between us. He didn't wash up after dinner. But nor did he complain about there not being enough food in the pot.

Meanwhile I went about my daily life feeling winded, but still upright. I consoled myself that Paul would go on living with us until the international borders opened up enough to make post-covid travel not just possible, but easy. He wasn't rejecting me, I reassured myself. He was choosing another way of life. He was choosing Italy over Australia. But then, one night before dinner, he suggested a walk during which he told me he'd taken over the lease on a friend's place nearby. This, for me, was the most painful moment of our separation. From one moment to the next, I realised that Paul wasn't leaving me for a more sympathetic life in Europe. He was leaving our home, which I knew he still loved, because he needed his independence from me even more.

That night at dinner, Paul broke his decision to Alex (Emma was living across the river by this point). 'I think that Helen', he said, 'will be better off without me.' I beg your pardon, I wanted to interrupt, but didn't. Instead I laid a pan of sausages and another of lentils onto the middle of the table. Then I did a mental doubletake. Paul made our separation sound like a comment on the weather, rather than, as it was for me, a firework in the sky that was setting the course for the rest of our life as a family. Sitting at the table, fork in hand, I felt hurt that I was no longer at the centre of Paul's universe. And as if this wasn't enough to be feeling, mixed in with this I also felt a bristling respect for his steely follow through.

Should I have seen this change of heart coming? I didn't. I had been too busy living – housekeeping, writing, mothering and teaching yoga – to see anything like this coming.

Even at the moment of pretending to eat dinner, I knew that Paul's return to live in Europe might be viewed as selfish by others. Yet I also knew, having known him for as long as I had, that his decision wasn't intended as a rejection of me, and that it was far more complex than simple selfishness. Moving out of our family home wasn't something that Paul wanted to do. It wasn't a daylight choice. It was something that he needed to do to save himself at a deep level, and despite everything – despite myself – I saluted him for it.

If I had to come up with a single explanation for why our marriage ended, depending on my mood I have several, it would be this. Our relationship ended as a result of Paul internalising me in a negative way. This happened ever so slowly. However once a tipping point was reached, that was it. Because ever after, whenever Paul glanced at me across the dinner table, or halfway up the stairs, he didn't see reflected back the man he felt himself to be. In the mirror of my face, he saw someone he didn't recognise, didn't want to be. This unconscious reaction to me seemed to happen no matter how much goodwill I felt for him, and showed him, in daily life. My mere presence made him feel complicated about himself, without my saying or doing anything. By the end, I didn't have to be in the house for him to feel it. And this, I think, is why Paul stopped loving me. It was like a chemical reaction that neither of us had wanted to mix up, but that once we had, neither of us had the power to reverse.

ℭℨ

Until his departure for Europe, Paul set up home in a neighbouring suburb. After decades of sharing a bathroom, he had his own everything. Every few weeks we had what we called a sandwich lunch, in which I dropped in on him after yoga class with sandwiches made by our favourite bakery which we ate in his sunny back room, talking about ideas with a simplicity that had been ours before life came along and changed our relationship so utterly.

So, what bearing does this twist have on my story about home life, apart from ruling out a conventional happy-ever-after ending? Well, it has everything but also nothing to do with it. It has everything to do with it because, as this story tells, over the years I've poured a huge amount of time, energy and love into home and family, and so this turn of events had to make me wonder about the value of doing so. But from a larger perspective, a kinder, non-judgy one, Paul's departure doesn't change my story that much. Because what I discovered, during this journey, is that while my love of a warm and pleasant home, clean spaces, shared meals and runner beans climbing up a pole, was awakened as a mother of small children, it no longer depends on having a family around all the time. I've never loved home work in any simple way. There are days when it drives me nuts, when it asks more from me than I have in me to give. I love it in a wholehearted way that I stumbled on as an effect of family life. Looking after my home, myself and those I love most is an important part of who

I am. And it was there, had I the eyes to see it, well before I had a family.

If I hadn't taken this journey, to the heart of home life, I may not have arrived at this conclusion. If I hadn't been prompted by my own experience of domestic conflict to tell this story, I might now be railing against an unjust universe and a selfish ex-husband. However, being on this path has shown me vistas, contours and grassy expanses that I mightn't have seen otherwise. So that when I look back on how I got to where I am now, I don't feel bitter. I feel moved to wonder at my life so far.

In a strange way, I find myself in a similar position to the one I was in before Paul and I married, when I privately decided that however my life turned out, whether or not we had children, it would turn out well. Decades later, I still feel this.

When you can't have what you want, Freud wrote, the answer is to want what you have. This is something of what I now feel. I have two great kids who come and go. I have a lovely house and garden, and a loyal dog who eats horrible things on the beach. I still get on well enough with Paul to feel in touch with him, and to talk openly about important matters despite our having parted. And there is time ahead for another door to open. I really do have these things. Admittedly my life has been more challenging since Paul left. Yet in my heart, which is where it matters, I feel better about life in my strange new normal.

Recently, I spent a long weekend gardening. As I dug, pulled and pruned, I felt myself reclaiming the garden. As morning light turned to dappled afternoon light, what for ten years had been our garden became my garden. With each new day, I saw the results of my efforts. Throwing myself into gardening, without knowing quite why or what I was doing, left me feeling braver, less fearful of my future.

Every morning, as I pulled on my jeans, I didn't relish the prospect of working in the garden. Yet by the end of the afternoon, as I pulled off my boots on the back doorstep, squashed in with the dog at my side, I felt hopeful about my life to come. Not in an ecstatic, 'this is so much better' sort of way. For I'd never have chosen to part with Paul. It was more the sense that if I could throw myself about the garden, if I could bend it to my shape and just keep on going, there was every reason to think that I could do other, equally hard things. With the light fading, as I looked around at the weeded grass and pruned-back plants, I needed no more proof of the value of the time, love and energy that I invested in home.

Sitting there on the doorstep, it came to me that, for the next while, I could do a Voltaire. I could keep on tending my garden, teaching yoga, writing and, once my son moved himself and his mountain of stuff out, rent out his part of the house. In the growing dusk, it struck me that, rather than setting off on a desperate quest to get what I wanted before it was too late, I could be even bolder. I could sit tight and let myself want what I already had. I could keep my sights on the path before me and make something of the way things were, released from the burden of trying to fix a marriage that couldn't be fixed.

This story, of my coming into awareness of the value of home work, of loving my home and family enough to care for them even when they didn't always appreciate my efforts, is one of the oldest in the world. But like all good stories, I had to live it for myself before I really understood it. Have I sacrificed myself in the telling? Perhaps, a little. (Others – including the feminist angel on my shoulder – might agree.) Then again, how could I have loved as much as I have, and for that long, without losing something? Besides I've also won hugely. Not least, I'm incredibly glad that I didn't see this plot twist coming, and that, for twenty-five years, I felt I was in a forever relationship.

14. green notebook

'Nothing is so bad that there's no good in it'
Finnish saying

Shortly before Paul left for Italy, my niece gave me a green notebook.
Each night as I lay in bed, before starting to read, I listed in it everything
I'd done that day. It was a simple thing. Yet just seeing written down the
main things I'd done each day served as proof that the earth is round and
not flat, and that my life hadn't come to an end just because Paul had
left it. While I never read these scrawlings back, I found them reassuring.
Paul had always traveled for work, so his absence from home wasn't new.
However knowing that he wasn't coming back felt different.

In the weeks and months that followed, I felt a groundswell of support
from friends and family. Even neighbours seemed friendlier. Our handyman took to knocking at the front door on flimsy pretexts, checking on
me. One weekend, unbidden, he brought around a chainsaw to chop in
half the stacked up logs by the gate so that they fitted inside my firebox. In
between sawing, and as I restacked the logs, he told me about his divorce
from years ago. Between the lines, his message seemed to be that his separation had turned out well and that, in time, mine might too. Then there
were days when, standing on street corners, acquaintances opened up to
me about their own break-ups, as if they'd happened yesterday.

At times I felt sad. But I was never only sad. I also felt relieved. And
lighter, definitely lighter. I kept a bottle of Ginseng in the cupboard just
in case, and had a deal with myself that if I felt depressed for more than
half a day I was to make an appointment with the psychologist I'd seen
with Paul. In the two years since Paul ended our marriage, I took Ginseng
a few times and saw the psychologist twice.

Mostly I threw myself into life, saying yes to everything that came my way. My son went on living in the cottage part of the house and my daughter dropped by now and then. I enrolled in an online design course and used it to turn around what had been our family house into my home. I sold my family grandfather clock and dining-room table to a dealer friend, after deciding that they'd have a better life with someone who loved them more than I did. I treated looking after my house and garden as a part-time job, which it is, and bought an electric whipper snipper to keep down the grass. I got my finances in order, sort of, overcoming my fear of book-keeping and of numbers in columns in general. I made an appointment with a lawyer to revise my Will and, at his prompting, wrote down in one place my every password and account number so that, should I disappear, my kids wouldn't be left to hunt them down. I went through cupboards and tossed out old towels and bedlinen that I'd stacked up awaiting for the fairies to mend them. And when the fences were replaced and six trees cut down at a neighbour's request, I bought hedging plants in small pots, partly for cost reasons but also because I knew enough about plants to know they'd be stronger for growing up in place. Every couple of months, I put two trestles together and invited ten friends for dinner because I didn't want to get out of practice. And while I loved being at home, I played with the idea of home exchange as a door to travel.

It wasn't all plain sailing. It took me a year to give up my sofa bed and return to sleep in the main bedroom. I struggled to play the piano, to draw and to sew, hobbled by 'what's the point?' taunts from within, and resorted to putting gold stars on a wall planner to mark my progress. (It sounds silly, I know, but it chimed with my inner 12-year-old.) I taught a lot of yoga, jumping in to cover classes whenever regular teachers couldn't. I put on a series of workshops to reality test my ideas about the home. And I walked my dog on the local beach, rain, gale or shine.

I'm not living the life that I was living when my mother died and left me with the question of whether she'd wasted her life. I live a different life now. Still, I feel quietly confident that if I can keep having good days, eventually they'll add up to a good life. Thankfully, Paul and I still have a lot of goodwill for each other, love even. We want each other's life to go well. Not surprisingly, our kids have taken longer to forgive us both, as would I if I were them.

An editor who read an earlier version of this story made the comment that it seemed to her that I'd put family and home before my relationship to Paul, and that readers may draw the awkward conclusion that my husband had left me for this reason. This made me squirm. Partly, of course, because this editor was right. Over time, I had put family and home before my relationship to Paul. What in our early years had been my singular love for Paul had turned, by an alchemy I'd been too busy to notice, into a bigger love for family and home inside which my love for Paul nestled. Even so, the idea that Paul left me because I loved home and family more than I loved him, well, I just couldn't wrap my head around that. It made no sense to me.

My intention, in this book, has been to tell the story of my unfolding relationship to home. While Paul was a good sport about his supporting role in it, I never set out to describe my unfolding relationship to him. Then again, and this is where it gets sticky, my aim in writing in the first person has always been to encourage readers to reach their own conclusion. And if my story unsettled this editor enough for her to feel that I might have seen the end of my marriage coming, and done something about it, all power to her.

One temptation, at the end of a long relationship, is to fall into what psychologists call the hindsight bias. Occasionally, I can feel myself ruminating along just these lines. Glancing back across the decades I can see, like a runway lit up at night, a trail of signs leading to Paul's departure. His lengthening trips to Europe. His growing circle of single friends. His dogged work hours. And yet I also know that these signs are tricks of the light and that, in reality, I was too caught up in the business of living to see more than a few months ahead. And I'm deeply thankful for that.

Also, now that I've had the chance to talk with scores of people about their feelings for home, I know that it isn't just me who feels as I do. Lots of people feel that their relationship to home is in some ways as important as their relationship to the people they live with and/or love most. Our home frames and gives rhythm to our day. It isn't some add-on that we can do without, as I learned all those years ago as an observer on a psychiatric ward. It's fundamental to who we are.

For many of us, home is a sanctuary from the world. Sometimes it's even a sanctuary from ourselves. It's a place where we can take refuge from our ego's noisy orders to get stuff done and to do ever better. The time that we spend at home gives us a break from being ourselves, from our grasping and striving and struggles to sit quietly alone in a room. With Adam Phillips, I now think that there are times when we are all too much for ourselves, when we're overwhelmed by feelings that we can't digest and that flood our defences, and that when we're taken up in this way, we're not in a position to meet the emotional demands that others make on us, no matter how much we love them. Every parent of a demanding child knows this. And, at certain moments, we're all this demanding child.

This makes home life, particularly family life, incredibly complex. This, in turn, explains our longing for simplicity. We long for clutter and dust-free spaces. We prize ordered cupboards and airy space in the wardrobe. We long to lose ourselves in states of flow, and to be rewarded by the contentment arising from them. And while we can't help seeking reassurance from others that our efforts at home are appreciated, in our hearts we know that we are the only ones who can truly value what we do there.

The morning that Paul shouted at me by the back door, holding a cafetiere in one hand and a laptop under his elbow, threatening the end of our marriage, I walked into the kitchen, flicked on the extractor fan light, got out the Gumption and scrubber and set about cleaning the hob. From the outside, this was my second Cinderella moment, confirming my incarceration at home. But from the inside, this was a grounding moment. I wasn't falling apart. I wasn't in denial. I was scrubbing the hob. Whatever did or didn't happen in my relationship to Paul, I would be scrubbing the hob, and housekeeping in general, for the rest of my life. And knowing this steadied me.

By this point in my life I didn't hate housekeeping. My resentment of it had shrunk from a rushing river to a small puddle that I could easily step over. Likewise, in a weird way that I couldn't quite grasp, I didn't hate Paul for wanting to leave me, for wanting out, any more than I hated myself for failing to make him love me forever.

☙

These days, when the weekend comes around, I make two loaves of bread. Lately I've been playing with different flours in the bowl. I might toast nuts or seeds, folding them into the dough once it's past its stickiness, and adding gluten if the flours seem to need it. When I pass through the kitchen, during the rest of that day, I'll wash my hands, take the dampened tea towel off the bowl, wet my hands and knead the dough. After replacing the tea towel, I'll wash my hands again and get back to my day. Early the next morning, I'll turn up the oven before taking the dog for a walk, in readiness to take the loaves on our return.

I love these early morning walks – the same old streets look new and bright, the plants and trees whispering of the season to come and of the one just passing. And I relish coming back into the house, later that morning, to the smell of fresh bread. Usually I keep one loaf for myself and give the other one away, wrapped warm in a tea towel. It just feels like the right thing to do. I stumbled on this rule in a letter from Carl Jung, and often find it useful. I do what feels like the next right thing – even when I don't feel like doing it, especially when I don't feel like doing it – and then the one after that. Later, when I look around, I can see where all these actions, added together, have taken me. The path that I'm on may not be straight, but it's definitely my path.

Initially I worried that my friends and family would feel sorry for me when they heard that Paul had left me. It felt such a raw thing to have to announce. But I soon realised that my fear was mistaken. Most of the people I knew were too wrapped up in the hurtling that we call life to dwell on my story for very long or in much detail. Then again, it could be that once they saw that I didn't feel sorry for myself, they didn't feel compelled to be sorry for me either. Or perhaps they were just being tactful, in giving me time and space to come to terms with the change.

These days, housekeeping accounts for more time in my day than it did when I lived in a small London flat and shopped with a list on my way home from the tube station. However because I feel less conflict around it, I think about it less. It takes up less space in my mind. That said, I'm still not a homebody. I need time away from home every day to appreciate the time that I spend there. Even as a young mother, I always felt drawn to something greater than home and family. Not feeling this pull towards a higher sense of purpose, however it's described, would have spelled insanity for me, and possibly for my family too.

Annoyingly, getting older hasn't made me wiser. Still, there are some things that getting further along my path have taught me. I now think that living life creatively – making new associations between ideas, and making the links between them wider and deeper – is more important than putting pressure on myself to be creative or have things to show for my creativity. Feeling creative at home is more like a conversation that I have with myself than it is a tick-list of must do's. Still, I do like to make and do things at home, and sometimes need to nudge myself to get into it. Recently, I've taken to bribing myself to sit down at the piano and to open my drawing pad. Similarly, when it comes time to garden, pulling on my old jeans and riding boots helps me over the mental block that seems to stand between me and the garden bed. I've also found that asking friends for dinner, when it's still a passing fancy, works better for me than waiting until I've had second thoughts about committing myself to cook. Finally, I've learnt that setting aside an hour each day for housekeeping, broken up or whole, suits me better than waiting for slots of time to offer themselves.

Nowadays, I treasure the gaps in my day. When I'm home at lunchtime,

I'll sit on the top step by the back door, plate on my knees, looking out at the garden, wedged in with my dog. Late afternoon, I'll lie in a yoga pose on the rug at the top of the stairs, digesting my most ordinary of days. I relish time to do nothing, and miss it terribly when I'm so busy that one thing butts against the next like too many boats in a marina. And, when I really don't want to do something, and there is no argument I can mount to persuade myself to do it, I'll trick my unconscious into it by doing whatever it is for a few minutes, and extending the time at a tip-toe from there.

Now that my days of mothering for a family of four are over, I have the benefit of hindsight. Luckily for me, I like not being needed nearly as much as I liked, for all those years, being needed. Looking back, it strikes me that what I lacked most, during those fairground years, was time. I'm aware that not everyone needs time to themselves. However for those of us who are sensitive, creative and, yes, selfish, family life can present an ongoing challenge. Meeting the emotional needs of our family, without having time to recover, is perhaps the most demanding work that we do as human beings.

A mother, and often a father, assumes many roles in relation to their growing children. Apart from the obvious roles, as cook, cleaner, driver and organiser, we're often mentor and coach too. In the most intuitive way, we create an atmosphere at home that encourages children to lose themselves in activities from which they emerge just a little stronger and more complex. Every day we encourage, elicit and give feedback to our kids in the hope that, when they grow up, they'll have the skills and sense of purpose to find their own way.

There is just one problem with this. Which is that, as parents, we need to lose ourselves in creative activities as much as our children do. Sadly, it's all too easy to fall into an arrangement, without anything being said, in which we give to our kids what we need for ourselves. Through our attentiveness to them, our kids receive the recognition, the nudging, the snacks and the distraction-free time that we also need. And yet, unless we're single-minded to the point of ruthless, most of us find it simpler – it incurs less emotional resistance – to encourage our children to be creative, than it is to find the time, space and energy to nourish our own creativity.

Family love is tiring. Day after day we have to overcome ourselves, our defences and even our laziness in order to do what's best for our family as a whole. Within the space of hours we make countless line calls. In some ways, being a parent is akin to being an octopus, with tentacles reaching out in all directions that keep everyone afloat and connected. Until one day, trust me it will arrive, it comes time to withdraw our tentacles. Our work as a parent isn't done. However, we have our tentacles to ourselves more often. And with the time, space and energy this frees up, we have the opportunity to reclaim our creativity once more.

This is what I didn't understand, in relation to my mother, when I was growing up. I took the dynamics between us very personally. Our conflicts were all about her and all about me. I wasn't able to step back and see the dynamic between us for what it was. I couldn't see that my mother was controlling because she lived in quiet fear of our home life toppling from within. So secure was I in her love that I couldn't see how overwhelming she found family life and yet how precious it was to her.

A few months ago, I took over the job of doing a weekly vase of flowers at the yoga studio I teach at. Initially I kept my flower arrangements modest. I kept a pair of secateurs in the pocket of my car door, a tip from my design course, so that I could snip flowers growing wild while out on long walks. Eventually, feeling cramped with what I could put in a small jug, I took in a larger jug from home so that I could play with bolder arrangements. My mother used to arrange flowers in a semi-professional way, growing flowers for that express purpose. My own attitude to arranging flowers is more relaxed than hers was and my gardening skills more limited. Still, I think that I've taken this love of flowers from her. Sadly, she isn't alive to see this change in me. Although, perhaps this is the way these things sometimes go.

This small gesture, of doing flowers at my yoga studio, has led me to look at the plant world with real interest when out walking my dog. My eye is drawn to yellow succulents on the roadside, red geraniums sprawling above a pebbly beach, white blossoms shading a coastal path, and purple echium spikes nodding unreachably high above it. I keep a bucket full of water by the front door in which I collect flowers and branches that I might use the following week. These flower arrangements, which in winter have more ivy and branches than flowers, are part of my home work. It's my way of flagging to the world that small gestures are valuable, and that when you stumble on something that you find satisfying, it's good to share it with others.

Ultimately this story has more to do with my relationship to my mother than with my relationship to my ex-husband. Not the woman who, after a country childhood, lived in four different streets in Adelaide, and who I lived apart from for the whole of my adult life. But the mother in my mind, the part of myself that I long struggled to own and that, when I did, made me the woman I now am. My mother's life is now recognisable to me in a way that it wasn't when all I wanted to do, needed to do, was to be independent of her, to be uninfluenced by her.

How was I to know, on first stepping off the plane in London in my early twenties, that it was because I'd been well loved and looked after as a girl that housekeeping would present itself as a struggle for me? How was I to know just how long it would take for me to unearth the fantasy, shared by countless others, that in my unconscious I was absolved of all domestic duties which, if they were done at all, were done by someone else, offstage? How was I to know that by the time I reclaimed my domestic instinct, by giving up my resistance against cleaning up after myself and by choosing to live my life whole rather than splitting it into parts that I expended precious energy keeping apart from each other, that I'd be facing down middle age with two children of my own? Yet this is exactly what happened.

These days, when I talk to younger people about the home, I feel immense sympathy. Their experiences will be different from mine and those of my generation. Still, the challenges they face will be similar: how to care about things in the here and now that ultimately aren't worth bothering about, how to turn a daily domestic assault course into something resembling an art form, how to overcome our resistance to doing loathed tasks, and how to hold in reserve enough love and energy for activities that, while we profess to love them, we tend to put off. Will the next generation, whether or not they have children, develop or suppress their longing for beauty at home? Will they, as I did, experience a conflict between how they'd like to feel at home, and what they fear they'll be made to feel (oppressed, overlooked, taken for granted) if they realise their fantasies of home?

There are good reasons why so many of us force the domestic side of ourselves into hiding for as long as we do. Society sends out messages which tell us to live in fear of sacrificing ourselves, our promise and our ambition, to home duties. We fear this so much that we risk splitting domesticity in two: into a home life that we moan about not keeping on top of, and a home life that we long for in fantasy. Dropping our defences and allowing our domestic side to surface is scary. Who knows where we would end up if we admitted openly to loving our home? It lays us open to feeling vulnerable, dependent, wishful and trivial. And yet, in my experience, this is how we become whole.

There will come a morning – a birthday – when we wake up to the second half of our life. How, we wonder, did *that* happen? This is often, as it was for me, a turning point, after which our defences start to crumble. Crafts, hobbies and activities that we had no time for in our twenties and early thirties become more appealing, more satisfying, even while knowing we may never be that good at them. We loosen our grip on master lists and five-year plans, and feel ourselves drawn to things and experiences that are satisfying in themselves.

We do that terrifying thing called settling down. Rather than holding out until we solve all our problems and find the perfect mate, we throw ourselves into the life that we find ourselves in the middle of. We don't welcome problems with open arms exactly, but we do recognise them as part of who we are. Knowing we may never be rid of them, we treat them as part of the landscape and so a little less seriously. Settling down frees us up. It allows us to start caring more deeply for things that we really do care about, and less about things, but for our desire for a warm and pleasant home, we might otherwise avoid (housework, maintenance, errands). We still feel a conflict between how we'd like to feel at home (relaxed, engaged, buoyant) and the price we have to pay to achieve it (domestic work). However because we live this dilemma daily, rather than apprehending it in the future, housekeeping comes to feel less burdensome, even interesting. This, anyway, is how it has unfolded for me. Looking after oneself and one's family will always be harder than being looked after by someone else. And yet in my experience it is less emotionally complicated, as well as more satisfying and rewarding.

Nowadays, the people I admire most aren't especially clever or famous. They're people who are good at the daily task of living. They're people who are able to juggle competing demands on their time, their affections and their work. Grace under pressure now seems more impressive to me than the ambition and IQ I esteemed above all else when I was younger.

So much of what we do at home comes down to our willingness to keep on going in the face of uncertainty. This, in essence, is what home work is for me. It's a daily expression of my willingness to do things that I don't really care about, for the sake of something bigger that I really do care about. For me, these big things are love and beauty. The kind of love that I've stumbled on goes beyond family, to everyone I care about. It extends to everyone I know who is in the throes of doing this difficult thing called life. This love, *agape* in Greek, is not better than romantic love. However it does feel different, less exclusive somehow. This love isn't something I chose to feel. It's something that found me out and changed me from within. Is it an effect of maturity? A little. But it's not just about the passage of years. It's also a choice that I made. Or that made me. Who can tell?

As I write this, I can hear the angel on my shoulder murmur that I was tricked into embracing domesticity when I had children and wanted to create a home for them. And that, had I not let my romantic love for Paul morph into family love, he might not have left me. What I tell this angel in reply is that this insight comes from outside the linen cupboard of my childhood, and that my whole purpose in this story has been to tell it from inside my heart, looking out. I've tried to describe home life from inside the linen cupboard, held aloft by feather doonas and an enveloping love that I've been lucky enough to receive. And, just perhaps, it's thanks to this expansive love that I've been able to take my place on the wheel of life in a way that, before this happened, for complicated emotional reasons I was unable to do.

These days, whenever I visit a friend, I take along something from my garden. A bunch of lavender, a handful of lemons, or any other flowers that happen to be out. These gifts are an expression of my love, and giving them gives me something important back. Looking after family and home, and all the care and creativity that went into that, didn't waste my mother's life any more than it is wasting mine. Clearly there is more to life than housekeeping. The world is a big and exciting place, and it's never too soon to get curious about what comes next. Still, it's a pretty important part. If my mother were alive today, I'd tell her about the vases of flowers and the lemons. And I'd say to her, 'See what you've given me? You've wasted nothing.'

my house rules

1. Make the bed each morning.

2. If a task takes a few minutes or less, do it straight away.

3. Whenever possible, touch things only once.

4. Attend to whatever it is as it arises.

5. Leave home in a state that makes me want to return to it.

6. Whatever household task I least want to do, do first.

7. Make or do something creative every day.

8. Try to do with grace what I have to do anyway.

bibliography

Ashenburg, Katherine, *The Dirt on Clean*, Farrar, Strauss and Giroux, 2007

Benjamin, Marina, *The Middlepause*, Scribe, 2016

Brown, Brene,
 Braving the Wilderness, Penguin, 2017
 I Thought It Was Just Me, Penguin, 2008

Burgo, Joseph, *Shame and Pride*, Pan Macmillan, 2018

Burkeman, Oliver, *The Antidote*, Text, 2012
 Four Thousand Weeks, Penguin, 2021

Csikszentmihalyi, Mihaly, *Creativity: The psychology of discovery and invention*, Harper Collins, 1996
 Flow: The classic work on how to achieve happiness, Random House, 1992

Esfahani Smith, Emily, *The Power of Meaning: The true route to happiness*, Penguin, 2017

Duras, Marguerite, *Practicalities*, Grove Press, 1987

Epstein, Mark, *Advice Not Given: A guide to getting over yourself,* Penguin, 2018

Flanagan, Caitlin, *To Hell With All That: Loving and loathing our inner housewife*, Little, Brown & Co, 2006

Gladwell, Malcolm, *Blink*, Penguin, 2006

Havrilesky, Heather, *What If This Were Enough?* Doubleday, 2018

Jane Hornby, *What To Cook And How To Cook It*, Phaidon, 2010

Honore, Carl, *The Slow Fix*, Collins, 2013

Kondo, Marie, *Spark Joy*, Penguin, 2016
 The Life-Changing Magic of Tidying, Random House, 2011

Jarski, Rosemarie, *Domestic Bliss: A modern guide to homemaking*, New Holland, 2006

Leslie, Ian, *Curious: The desire to know and why your future depends on it*, Basic Books, 2015

Lethbridge, Lucy, *Servants*, Norton, 2013

Light, Alison, *Mrs Woolf and the Servants*, Penguin, 2007

Lush, Shannon & Fleming, Jennifer, *Speed Cleaning*, ABC Books, 2006

Magnusson, Margareta, *The Gentle Art of Swedish Death Cleaning*, Scribe, 2017

Marcal, Katharine, *Who Cooked Adam Smith's Dinner?* Scribe, 2015

Mendelson, Cheryl, *Home Comforts: The art and science of keeping house*, Cassell & Co, 2001

Milner, Marion, *A Life of One's Own*, Virago, 1986

Morrow Lindbergh, Anne, *Gift From the Sea,* Hogarth Press, 1985

Samin Nosrat, *Salt, Fat, Acid, Heat*, Penguin, 2017

Phillips, Adam, *On Balance*, Penguin, 2011

   Going Sane, Penguin, 2016

Ploeg, Inge van der, *Clear the Clutter,* Floris Books, 2004

Rapinchuk, Becky, *The Organically Clean Home*, Adams Media, 2014

Setiya, Kieran, *Midlife: A Philosophical Guide,* Princeton, 2017

   Life is Hard, Princeton, 2022

Tatsumi, Nagisa, *The Art of Discarding,* Hachette, 2017

Ware, Bronnie, *The Top Five Regrets of the Dying*, Hay House, 2012

Milton Keynes UK
Ingram Content Group UK Ltd.
UKHW041951031123
431812UK00001B/39

9 781922 571915